ANGELS EXPLAIN God AND THE NEW SPIRITUALITY

Cheryl Gaer Barlow

Also by

Cheryl Gaer Barlow

Angels Explain Death and Prayer

ANGELS EXPLAIN GOD AND THE NEW SPIRITUALITY

Cheryl Gaer Barlow

LIGHT Technology PUBLISHING

For more information about special discounts for bulk purchases, please contact Light Technology Publishing Special Sales at 1-800-450-0985 or publishing@LightTechnology.net

* * *

ISBN-13: 978-1-62233-023-2

Light Technology Publishing, LLC
Phone: 800-450-0985
928-526-1345
Fax: 928-714-1132
PO Box 3540
Flagstaff, AZ 86003
www.LightTechnology.com

Contents

Now is the time to search and sort;
to throw away all desires not of your highest ideals and strongest inspirations;
to understand the meaning of your being, the purpose of your hopes;
to gravitate to your purest thoughts; and
to cherish the stainless beauty of your visions and all in your life that is heavenly.

Aspire to all the greatness that is you
and pour out the torrents of strength encased in your soul.
You will find there is no end
except the calmness and peace of blessed accomplishments.
Many times, you have thought and dreamed,
and you cherish those dreams.
But now is the time to put away
the little losses, the angers, the sadness, the doubts,
and all that does not measure up to your perfect potentiality.

Stand in the highest realm of
all the goodness and glory you can partake,
and take upon yourself
the regeneration of the world.

— Cheryl Gaer Barlow

There are souls walking Earth who are among the highest, most caring, and most gracious. Not only am I relating the sacred messages from the holy angels of God, but I'm also honored to have these souls as part of my life as my dearest friends and family. It's to these great souls I dedicate this book.

The Message of This Book

From the Angels: The message of this book is to tell the souls of Earth about the wonders of God, the glorious angels, the heavens, the Earth, and all existence. Know above all things that God loves you more than any words can express.

God will welcome you to the heavens at your life's end, no matter what has happened in this life. We angels are always with you, and we love you more than you could ever conceive. The wonders of the heavens await all on Earth.

The words given in this book are the true words of the Angels of the Mallbon. Cherish these words and do not doubt them as truth. The mentions within are the eternal words from the heavens. If the souls of Earth knew of the wonders surrounding the one God, they would pray incessantly with a crying heart and plead to be in audience with the angels.

People would beg to God with tears of joy for the forgiveness of their lowly ways. The people of the world want to know a way to lift to God. Herein, we express the ways to merge with the heavenly entities. Make your life the wonder you desire. Live a life you would be honored to show God.

The Holy Bible

From Cheryl: Many of the truths given today from the angels may conflict with biblical teachings because the Holy Bible has gone through many translations by humankind, which included misinterpretations, ignorances prevalent at varied times, and varied languages, rendering it inaccurate in some aspects. The Holy Bible was a valid writing for its day, but it has gone through many changes to engage the masses into a fear of God rather than a love of God.

When a message is translated into varied languages, care must be taken to keep the message intact. What is read in the Holy Bible is good or not good, depending on the verse. Much will be revealed through varied writings coming forth into the world.

The angels say the Holy Bible is not to be taken literally. Writings were from many men who were visited by angels and took the whisperings and perceptions as their own. Their words were taken as the truth. Some added their own thoughts and impressions. This was the time of storytelling, and some tales were embellished.

As writings were compiled, leaders of the church councils took out any reference they felt would not keep the populous bound to the religion. Directives were given to instill fear in the followers so that they would not stray from the church teachings. The words were changed to bring the masses to the church. No one questioned these, as this was the only spiritual connection. These words were adapted as the entire truth of all things.

Skepticism

From Cheryl: This book is filled with sacred messages from the holy angels of God. Of this, I have no doubt. I've come to understand, from the reactions of learned people whose opinions I honor, that there are those who hesitate to believe that I (or anyone) can receive words from angels. Some simply do not believe that anyone on Earth has ever seen an angel, been touched by an angel, or been spoken to by an angel.

Prejudice exists that any communication with a heavenly creature is comparable to that of a soothsayer or false prophet or that it is akin to channeling devils, spirits, fairies, and the like. They might react in complete disdain for what they consider to be occult, supernatural, mystical, or psychic hocus-pocus.

Angels communicate both in an inner, subjective way and with an acute, outer, objective phenomenon. Angels are with us always to help and guide and whisper truths. The words come when I'm ready to receive them, exclusive of any trance state. It's completely natural, as if they are sitting beside me dictating the words. Nothing of the book is created from my own mind. I'm a scribe, nothing more.

The words of the angels are sound, wise, sustained, thought provoking, and intelligent, which undermines any assumption of a disorder, dysfunction, or mental deterioration. These thoughts are clearly distinguishable from my own: "We are the holy angels of God. Now is the time to write the book of our sacred words." When phrases such as these come into your consciousness, you know they are not of your own making. Some feel communication with angels is an abnormal perception. They feel these can only be perceived by a mind with a mental condition — delusional, psychotic, illogical, erratic. Some might think any mind believing these words is weak, disorganized, under the influence of mind-altering substances, or in pursuit of recognition to enhance one's self-worth.

Some may assume these revelations are made up from my own mind or from an altered state. These are assumptions I would probably make too had I not experienced the angel myself — felt her touch, heard her words, and encountered other unexplained phenomena.

This is beyond moral certainty. This is positive proof of the existence of heavenly entities. This angel visitation wasn't a faint, translucent figure in the corner of a darkened room. This was an intense, brilliant, in-your-face, all-encompassing event unlike anything I'd ever experienced! It was not a dream, a vision, or a hallucination. It was not supposed or imagined. It was not fiction. This was true, real, and authentic.

I'm open to the possibility this may be a predisposed, genetic trait because many tales of angelic visitations were handed down through the family line. A questioning mind could dismiss this as unscientific, but I feel the perceived realizations of today will be tomorrow's scientific findings. The messages for humankind are active and profound.

Some will read this now only to find that the angels' words disagree with a lifetime of teachings. Those open to the spiritual will understand the words of the angels. I realize that not all who read this will believe. The angels have told me that I will be mocked, ridiculed, and demeaned. It's good to question information before acceptance. To mimic and scoff are not solutions to rejection. To try to make another opinion seem ignorant is not a way of understanding. I don't believe all truths are merely revealed but are given by varied means.

Some will not accept or understand these writings, and it's not my intention to offend any existing beliefs. To undermine others' sacred beliefs is to hurt the soul, for this is what they grasp onto to make sense of the world and their place in it. I ask you to read these words from the holy angels of God with an open mind and heart.

Preface

From Cheryl: Universal Intelligence, Providence, the Old Man in the Sky, the Big Boss Upstairs, Him — as you sheepishly point to the heavens, you use these names instead of the word "God." Why do people shy away from using the word "God"? Why are people shocked when you say the word "God" aloud? Any other description of God seems acceptable but not the word itself. Does saying "God" mark you as a religious fanatic? Is God so far above those of us on Earth that the name can't be spoken aloud? Does the word "God" invoke embarrassment? Since many feel they are agnostics or atheists, is it incorrect to say God?

I'm not a religionist. Actually, I quit the church as a child, never to return. Were it not for a holy angel of God appearing to me in an intensely brilliant light, reaching out and touching me on the forehead, and telling me I had been chosen to bring the words of the angels to the world, I probably would have been shrouded in skepticism. Having blind faith or following a belief because someone said it was so was not my idea of logical, intelligent reasoning.

The angel didn't appear a vision or an apparition. The angel's visit was not a dream nor a hallucination. The light encompassing the room was intensely blue-white. The angel floated in on its shaft, which entered through the window. After entering, she was at first translucent, and then she became as a solid, flesh-and-blood person before my eyes. Her face was lovely, her hair was long and wavy, and her gown was white with hints of lavender. She explained to me as she glided about that I was to bring the words of the holy angels of God to the world. This is the reason I was born on Earth, and it is something that I agreed to before my birth.

How would you react if this happened to you? I'd like to think I looked like a lady in a beautiful Renaissance painting, silent and serene. Not me! I tried to speak, but no sound came out. If an utterance occurred, I'm sure it was a gasp, more like the sound of a wounded walrus! She, however, was all beauty, luminosity, and loveliness. She spoke in the softest voice and touched my forehead in a gentle, graceful movement. This lasted about fifteen minutes. After she and the light disappeared, I sat up the remainder of the night staring into space. "What just happened?"

I have experienced other extraordinary happenings throughout my life. This visitation was not supposed, not imaginary. This was not conceived of my own thought. The words were and are rational, practical, wise, and sustained. I've evaluated this phenomenon from varied perspectives, and it remains: The words of the angels of God come to me whenever I'm ready to receive them.

I write the words at the same time I "feel" them without deciphering meaning or content at the time. I can think of a question, and it's answered for me. The words come as between a whisper and a thought. I'd hear, "Cheryl, the time is now for you to write our books. This is why you were born on Earth at this time. We are the holy angels of God." There was no relenting, no getting away from what was agreed on.

Angel Sightings

The angels have come to me through sightings or sound over the years. However, I'll relate one instance in which I couldn't see my angel, but my children could. Children, unfettered by the years of living on Earth in physical bodies, easily perceive these images.

When my children were three and four years old, I was fixing breakfast for them in my sunlit kitchen. "I'll be right back," I told them as I ran up the stairs.

When I ran back down, my son said, "Mommy, There's a lady all dressed in white behind you. She followed you upstairs and back down."

It's my angel! I thought. "You see her too?" I asked my daughter.

"Yes," my daughter nodded her head up and down. "Yes, Mommy, she's right there!" pointing behind me.

At last, I'll get to see my angel again. I turned around, seeing only the table, the flowers, the window, and the refrigerator. My heart fell. Why can't I see through the eyes of a child? Other times, I've seen angels either in a whitish, detailed outline or as a translucent figure. At times, they have been so clear and real that I've had to step back.

Coming from a sweet, quiet Scandinavian/Welsh family in a small Montana town, I understood I must not tell the world of these sightings. This is something to be whispered to the relatives as a hushed secret, lest I be locked in a rubber room. But when a holy angel of God asks you to do something, can you refuse? I didn't refuse but delayed this as long as possible. Any mention of it was responded to with scorn, mocking, ridicule, and even hatred. I've been shunned by friends and called the devil, and I even had a salad thrown at me. Why would anyone subject him- or herself to that?

The words from angels were unrelenting. I wrote them exactly as received with no infusion of my own beliefs. There's nothing occult about this. It's as natural and normal as talking to a friend. By completing this book, I have summoned the courage to bring you the words of God's holy angels. No words of Earth could begin to explain the infinite, holy God. The angel's words are the closest but are mere shadows of the true explanation.

Bringing All into Perfection

For centuries, lore has been passed down through biblical writings, churches, and storytelling to give us a better understanding of God and Jesus and how they came into being. I know that in a different century, I'd probably be tortured for these words, as they differ from messages siphoned from known writings.

Now, from the angels, I'm given new knowledge about the birth of Jesus, of God, and of the Holy Spirit. I understand this information will not be freely accepted, but I'm obligated to bring the words of the holy angels of God exactly as received.

The world is a creation of God. All things are creations of God. God himself is his own creation. This is all created from thought manipulating the energies. God is not a stagnate entity. God's works are perpetually growing and changing, expanding in culture, intelligence, formation, and creativity. This is a way to explain the one God, as he is multiplying in his effects. There is continuous change and growth, ceaseless re-creation.

In the stratum of eternal being, God goes beyond the constant, the everlasting, which is forever. This is the realization of pure consciousness into perpetual growth. It is not the change of people on Earth reflecting the level into a series of transformations but rather bringing all into perfection, the attainment of all development.

God envelops all and is forever open to all ways of growth. God created himself and all beings, all form, and all matter. God created the gods and all entities of the heavens and all worlds. All is God's creation — all.

Only God and the Holy Spirit were in existence. This is the everything. All life sprang forth from this wisdom and light.

In the Presence of Angels

I'm sure people will ask if I'm trying to change the Holy Bible. No, I'm not — nor do I wish to offend anyone's belief system. If these messages were received from spirits on Earth, I would agree they are probably false. However, these are sacred messages from the holy angels of God as they watch over Earth. I ask only for the highest angels to come to me. When one of these holy angels enters the room, I stand, overwhelmed at the sudden serenity and enveloping compassion. At times, my eyes tear from the fullness of the heart. My eyelids tingle, sometimes so intensely that I can hardly keep them open.

It's then that I'm my true self — a naked, trembling soul, aware of being in a presence so profound and so powerful — and I must gather strength before I can speak. Yet I need not speak, for she knows my thoughts, feelings, and fears. So I stand in disbelief of the gentleness of love blanketing me, awed to know the highest, purest, most holy of entities is watching over me, standing before me, beckoning me to feel God's love.

I struggle for words. I fall in surrender, swept in a whirlwind of tenderness. In a shaky, squeaky voice, I whisper, "Thank you."

I know these are clarifications and additions to religions of the past. People tend to stand by documents of long ago. When new knowledge is unfolded on Earth, people tend not to believe it. Once they truly open their hearts to God, they will know these words are the truth. What follows are the words of angels.

CHAPTER ONE

Communicating with the Angels

From Cheryl: Writing to your angels is a powerful act, often creating tremendous results! It's said that Mark Twain used letter writing to receive telepathic results. He would write the letter, feeling the emotions of what he wrote, and then tear it up, saying that writing the letter was the essential thing. In a few days, he would receive a response from the particular person he had written to with the desired information. Writing focuses thoughts into a deliberate, clear, forceful act of thought transference. How much more powerful do you think it is to write to a celestial being?

Write to Your Angels

Angels are God's emissaries at work on Earth. You need only to be aware of our presence, for we surround all souls. We may appear or not appear, be heard or not heard, but know that angels are with you this second. We know more about you than you know of yourself. We don't judge or punish. We guide, help, and understand. Let us into your life. You will be accepting of the spirituality surrounding you when the time is right and when circumstances usher you to know.

How do I communicate with angels?

Writing messages helps solidify thought to make desires specific. It propels the movement of your soul into a movement of the atmosphere, moving the written thought into action. Putting the written thoughts to paper also organizes and clarifies your intent.

Angels know your thoughts and your feelings. Thoughts are often not sustained. Ask your highest angels to surround you. Speak to us as if you would speak to a friend. We hear and understand. If you write to us, we stand with you and read your words. We help in whatever ways are possible.

Can we write to angels surrounding other people?

Yes, it is accomplished as requested. Whoever is asked will come forth to receive messages. We bring wellness and compassion to souls. Writing to angels will be read and understood. We can better assimilate the focused desires.

Angels of the Mallbon

We have lived lives upon lives in many worlds. When we were ushered to meet God, he knew the love in our souls. He appointed us to the status of holy angels of God. Many realms of angels exist. We are in the heavens and in all worlds. It is a great honor to be appointed to the status of an angel.

We choose the realm we wish to inherit. Angels help with different growths of the soul and have varied interests and pursuits. No discipline is given, for we are all in perfection. Some choose to master entitlements. Some serve God. Some stay with the heavenly gods. Some move through the worlds. We have chosen to watch over the souls of Earth because the souls here are most needy.

We are God's most sacred angels in all realms. We hold more empathy than can be described. We guide souls to God. We help in whatever ways we can. We lift the souls at the end of life in the body. We listen. We watch. We know the feelings of all the souls we cherish. The angels in all realms are all light and love. We hold more tenderness because the people of Earth are most fearful.

Many worlds begged us to watch over the higher souls. We chose Earth because we can be of more help on this lower world. As we are appointed to enter the order of the Mallbon Angels, a most sacred ceremony is bestowed upon us. This is felt in all the heavens. The glory of it is unlike any feeling we have experienced in all our thousands of lives.

The Mallbon Angels hold a deeper compassion than any other

angelic realm. We are always near the souls of Earth. We could even touch you and you would not be aware of our presence. We are visible and not visible, heard and unheard. We may appear as any person on Earth. We may speak with you, and you are not aware you are speaking to an angel. We may dress and speak as any soul of Earth.

We have chosen you as our charges. We knew you before your birth on Earth and asked to be your guardians. As we watch your souls grow and develop, we are exalted. At the end of your life, we will lift you to the heavens. We always protect your souls. We answer only to God. We do not serve humankind. We serve only God. When a word of God is given, we honor this.

All humankind is to give awareness to us. We are not from a sacrament of old. We are here and alive! Our souls differ from people's souls. We hold the light of God within us and are not without God at any moment. We can work miracles on Earth if it is deemed the best way to enact change. We usher prayers to God. Should God delegate the prayers to the guardians, we meet and discuss the fulfillment. If people knew the multitudes of ways we help them, they would bow and beg to us every moment of their lives. We do not desire this. We revel at the elevation of the soul.

Angels are everywhere on Earth. We surround the souls, bringing solace. Other realms exist as well as other orders of angels, all serving God in their own way. Only the Angels of the Mallbon give the qualities of tenderness, compassion, and love to humans' hearts. Other sects perform varied actions deemed by God. Any angel, rest assured, will cherish the requests from God. We will remain angels always and forever. We hold a high status, as do all in the heavens. We are glorious and of the love of all that exists.

Can you tell me more about the Angels of the Mallbon?

The love we emit is beyond comprehension. We are entities of light and love, and we can appear or disappear. We can become as humans on Earth or fly like birds. We work in ways unknown to humankind. We enact wonders and sooth pain and sadness. The tenderness we give is softer than most can receive.

We can influence events on Earth— even work miracles — and we lift the souls into the heavens. We are the holiest of all angel forces. We know your thoughts, your fears, and your desires. We cherish you and are your guardians. The lives on Earth would no longer exist were it not for our influences.

The mind can picture us as sylvan, but we are whole, perfect, and real angels of God. We are the love of the universe. We live in the heavens and are one with God. We bring God's directives to Earth. We are the most sacred of all the angels' realms.

We are the angels of God, and we are not without God at any moment. The most wonderful directives are given to us, as we have powers for miraculous events. We overlook our charges on Earth to help the growth of the soul and give protection to them. We weigh prayers as to worth and give the solemn prayers to God. We convene to deliberate the ways of enacting directives.

Are angels male, female, or both?

Angels, archangels, and all entities of the heavens are either male or female. Any sayings other than this is incorrect. We hold the light of God. Any entities other than male and female are at a soul's request and found only on Earth or in the hells.

Are there male and female angels around each person, and if so, why?

A life on Earth may require varied angels at different growth levels. This is done. The angels choose who they wish to mentor. Each soul has both male and female angels around it. Great souls can also bring gods to their being. These are either male or female. Angels realize the souls worth and do not discriminate in regard to gender. Angels gravitate toward fallen souls they can help.

In regard to the term "fallen angel," it denotes one who has fallen from grace. This does not exist. Each angel appointed by God will remain in this most holy state through eternity. We are in bliss with all qualities and all powers given to us by God. We seek no other existence but to serve God. This is a wonder of God to be the sacred Holy Angels of the Mallbon. Know we are with you at every moment.

Spirits on Earth

Are spirits to be heeded as angels?

Spirits only want to live again and wander Earth in search of anyone who may react to them. Give no credence to low spirits. Give them no worth, and they will depart. Be not afraid of them, for they hold no power. We angels are always with you. No one is ever to be afraid. Spirits may speak to you on Earth through thought, but they are not always true words.

We are appointed by God to become holy angels. Human spirits are not holy angels. They may seek to communicate with people of Earth but not with God's permission. We weld the glories of heaven in human minds. Spirits walking Earth have no power to do that. When a lower spirit enters the human mind, gather strength to force it away, and it will depart. The angels will protect you from this communication if you request it.

What powers do the spirits on Earth possess?

Spirits on Earth can work sounds. They can fly. They can move objects. They are not able to take your soul. They cannot take over your personality or individualism. When a person is under the influence of drugs or alcohol, the spirits can influence the mind so the person behaves and speaks irrationally; the person is not in complete control.

Morbid influences can affect the mind through fear and confusion. The spirits walking Earth have no other powers except to sometimes be visible to the human eye. They have no light of God in them. They wander Earth. The angels bade them to the heavens, but they refused. They are souls who wished to remain on Earth in spirit form.

CHAPTER TWO

Hell and Beings of Darkness

Does hell exist?

Yes, there is a hell. It's a magnificent place full of gods of darkness. The place you call hell is not a fiery place of agony. Many levels of hell exist where every desire of the mind is manifested. You can create your desire only for your own pleasure, not for another's. The higher hells are more beautiful than Earth. The lower hells are dark and reclusive. No light of God can penetrate the hells.

It's also a place of the most morbid followers. The people who choose to live in hell are followers of the ways of darkness. No one of God shall enter the hells unless he or she has begged through many lives to enter other than the heavens. The soul will have entrance to hell only after many lives of debauchery and morbidness, the many ways to God have been rebuked, and the angel's pleas have been discarded.

All desires are given in hell. These are not desires a person of goodness and love would want. These are desires of a lowly soul. Only people of ignorance or of evilness would desire to acquire these mentions. All things acquired in hell are kept through eternity. Hell is beautiful and magnificent in their eyes, and they will stay there forever.

These souls will not want to leave to be on Earth or on another world. All who leave Earth to enter hell are to be as gods in hell. They have powers of creation as well as other powers designated by the dark spirit. They live in luxury and are given anything they desire. They may not leave hell unless requested by the dark force, but they can request to serve him in other ways.

Those who choose hell don't experience joy and love as followers of God do. They will instead be unsatisfied with their belongings, ever searching for true happiness. Although a soul entering hell will live as a god, it will not experience the ecstasy reached in God's heaven. Neither pain nor agony will be in this place, but no creation will occur except for what each soul desires for itself. It's a place of opulence and satisfying one's own desires.

The place of the dark force is not a place worthy of the creations of God. God's children are all worthy to be in God's heaven. Open your heart and soul to God. The ways to reach God are many. If you are introduced to and reject all ways to reach God, there is no other way but the way of the dark spirit. This is a most regrettable way to follow. Lift your soul to God to be lifted to the heavens. Why would you want the ways of the dark spirit when God's heavens are open to you?

A Place of No Joy

What is it like in hell?

The opulence of hell can excite the senses of the lowest thought forms. People of no morality will be enticed to follow these ways. The gods of the hells or underworld delight in bringing souls to these places.

Hell is not a physical place as you experience on Earth. It is a creation of the mind. Thought forms the material world. This is real to the one experiencing it, but it's not real to those on a heavenly plane. It's looked at as a form of insanity, for there is neither goodness nor happiness.

Many pleasurable desires are given in the hells, but no true happiness will ever be experienced. No tears will form from happiness. No tingles of the soul will bring love into the heart. The entity will know of no happiness as experienced in the heavens. Hell is not a place of joy.

There are places in hell where the lowest carnal activities are indulged. Animalistic and abominable acts are indulged. There are no illuminations of the soul, no ennoblements of the spirit. It is a coarseness of the senses beyond imaginings. There is no growth, no possibility of lifting into God's light or God's blissfulness. It is corruption and evilness of the lowest. Hell has many faces and many realms. As the soul descends into darkness, wonders of God are closed to all eyes.

A soul is not to enter the hells on a whim, for it is eternal. The soul will sink lower and lower into dismalness and despondency. Even though the powers of creation are given to the soul, it gains no joy. The soul takes pleasure in manipulation and seduction of the most perverse actions a soul can perform.

Do not enter this in loose, diminished mental capacities. Build strength of thought, mind, heart, and feelings. Do not succumb to enter the hells at any life. Promises may be made of powers beyond what is now known on Earth, but hell is a place of no joy. Do not imbibe of what will distort thought and quench the feelings in the heart. Do not build hate or fear in the mind. Wonders beyond imaginings reside in the heavens. Lead people into the heavens for glories inconceivable.

I've always been taught that hell was a place of torment and terror. Could you clarify this?

There is no growth, no possibilities of lifting into God's light or God's bliss. There is corruption and evilness of the lowest. Many are enticed to see and feel this, but know this is not for a godly soul. When this path is chosen, the ways of God have closed on you. We issue a warning not to choose this path, for the ways to God are open for you to enter. Soar into the heavens.

Is there everlasting punishment?

No, you can't experience that. You will be given many ways to obtain God. When you have rejected God in all ways, you follow the ways of the dark spirit. This is only after many lives. Then you will live as a god of darkness with many strengths, except against God, the Father in heaven. Don't be afraid that the dark spirit will take you. This will only be a choice of the soul after many mentions of God are not followed.

Sin

What is sin?

Sin is a moral deviation. You are not punished by God for your sins. You punish yourself for your sins. Sin is what you perceive as not right action. With sin, you're doing what you think might hurt someone. You are not to hurt others, and you are not to be hurt, either.

People have the capacity to do what they want. They are not alone because we are always with all souls on Earth. All the angels try to help in the decision making, but it's not always accepted. Sin is a preplanned action of the lowest functions of the mind. This is what is perceived by the mind and soul as being against goodness, correctness, or right action. This is not to be arranged with preplanned forethought. People err enough without planned sin.

The soul is aware of all thought of the mind to continually choose to do wrong. To lie, cheat, steal, kill, or maim — whatever is not the way of God — keeps the mind in the lowest consciousness level. This is not the natural movement of growth for the mind and soul. The way of God is necessary for the growth of humankind. Live in the highest quality of thought.

Did Adam and Eve commit the first sin on Earth?

Sin lies within each person's mind. The Children of God were given a mission on Earth. They fought to survive and lived with the knowledge of God. These souls were of greatness.

The stories as told were not correct. The genesis souls on Earth were not as one would find people today on Earth. To men and women as these, the commitment of a mention against God was not conceivable.

The Children of God were as gods and goddesses. They honored God through the mortal life on Earth. They were not created out of the dust of Earth, nor did they knowingly sin against God in the heavens. The first on Earth were with God in their minds and their hearts. This was the beginning of the new world.

Is homosexuality a sin?

A soul may request a body for sexual exploration. However, many with these tendencies prefer to remain in the spiritual state, as they are not comfortable in a human body. Be tolerant of all growths of the soul, even if it is seemingly stagnant. The lower urges of the physical are indulged on Earth and in the hells. Sexual deviations are indulged as well. Whatever the soul desires is given. Try to understand the urges and desires — they are in the growth of the soul and are not to be judged but by God.

Entities in the heavens and on higher worlds are only male and female. Earth is the lowest world before entrance to the hells. An indulgence of sexual experimentation is prevalent on Earth, as people are new to experiencing the human form. We understand the affections, the lusts, and the ways of souls with these behaviors. These are deviant behaviors in other worlds where people are in physical bodies. Sexual desires are not acts that lead to God but are part of the lowly, cruder expressions of some souls.

The soul may go through many experiences before beginning the growth toward God. It is not for anyone on Earth to censor desires of any soul. Disregard what you feel are sins, and grow to God in your own soul.

The soul may desire deviation from what is considered "normal" on Earth. This is indulged. The plans for the life are made from an eternal perspective. The soul may want to experience a different life than has been known. These are deviations to be experienced when in a human body, if desired, but are not ordained by God. We don't judge the actions of the souls on Earth.

Anytime a soul feels love for another, that feeling grows in the heart. Any caring for another soul brings a tenderness to the heart. The gentleness helps the opening of the soul. Any love shared is a giving of oneself in this feeling, even if not reciprocated, and brings an opening of the heart of the soul.

Earth holds movements of love in all levels of creation. If it is only from the lower expression or from a deviation of expression, it is still a step toward soul growth. Men who love other men (or women who love other women) will still grow through love to reach God. Love begins with love for other humans until it becomes a love for God.

Carnal lust is not to be mistaken for love. When a deviant love (one that feels unnatural to the soul) is indulged, it is an expression to move away from God. This will not be open to misinterpretation. Deviant love is not a growth to God. People are to be who they are but use their capabilities to grow to God in all ways.

Is prostitution a sin?

Sexual urges are inherent in the physical body. To prostitute the body is not a sinful action, but it is also not a way to God. Moving the soul toward God can put sex into perspective. It's a natural physical urge of the mortal body. This is not to be looked at as a wicked method against God, for all are on God's path. You should try to keep the body in an order of respect and dignity. This will carry forward to cleanliness and dignity of the garment. These are all reflections of the growth of the soul.

The human body is given to the soul to be used as desired, but you should treat yourself with a high respect. This mortal body is not to be used as a lowly object. It's an honor to be in a human body. This is the clothing of your most sacred soul. The body is an expression of the soul and is to be used in a manner worthy of the self and as a Child of God.

Each of you is on your own path to God. Some are deterred and may not reach God as quickly as others. These should be tolerated as being on a detoured path. On Earth, all modes of growth do not develop in a balanced continuation. The intellect may grow in a steady movement, or the physical may attain constant growth. At times, the soul's heart may open and expand, or the sexual may move in a faster growth than the mind. The sexual feelings may, for a time, outweigh the discriminating or intellectual movements.

Is adultery a sin?

Each soul knows what is right in its own mind. In adultery, if it is only sexual, it's a lowly action. Lowly actions are not sins, but one should strive to have the highest possible thoughts and actions. One should always try to do what is right. Adultery for excitement is not correct action. Hurting any other soul is not right action.

"Sin" is a word to describe wrong or ignorant action purposely performed. One should try to make the existing relationship better rather than seek another. A wise man will wait until no one is hurt from that action. Risings of emotions will stir within, but a person of maturity will resist those emotions.

Not all people wed the true love of the soul. When this occurs, they may meet their true loves at another time. Lives go on through eternity. Love goes on through eternity. Doubts and confusion may be your angels giving warning. Caution should be given before marriage.

If you are in a marriage and unhappiness is the normal feeling, you should try to leave the marriage as easily as possible. Adversity will occur, but one should try to remember the good moments and the love. Treat each other with respect and courteousness with the least amount of anger.

Is thinking an evil thought as bad as actually doing the bad thing?

The thought in the mind and the performed action are two different things. You can think a thought but hold back from performing it. This shows a beginning of strength and discernment in the mind. As you evolve, the thought and performance of the action will become the same as each thought and action comes into perfection. On Earth, this is not easy to achieve, as thought is weak and not sustained. Whether the action performed is right or wrong is known in the mind. If it is perceived as wrong in the mind, the reaction or repercussion would also be perceived in the mind. The thought becomes strong and unwavering as the soul evolves.

It will become more difficult to perform what is considered a sinful, or wrong, action. First, the soul thinks the thought and performs the act. As the soul grows, it thinks the thought but thinks better of performing the act. As the consciousness merges with God, all thought and performance are in complete harmony with all life. It then is not possible to perform an evil act. The mind is above comprehension of an evil thought.

Is it all right in God's eyes to sin?

While the soul of the mortal is in ignorance, it knows no better. Once you understand right and wrong, you bear the burden of what *you* interpret as sin. This will be in the soul's remembrance. You will hold this to yourself as part of your consciousness. This will keep you in a place not close to God until you can release this and no longer punish yourself. When the mind knows correct action but chooses to do the opposite, this keeps you from attaining your goals.

A soul will place itself in the heavens, as it will feel repentance for its actions. It will be humbled as it becomes aware of the exulted souls in the heavens. The wonders await each of you in any heavenly home you choose. You will hold no arrogance. You become aware of the growth that must occur.

Angels of Darkness

Was the story of Jacob wrestling the angel [in the Book of Genesis] a literal translation?

The words of the Bible are not to be taken literally. The angels are of God and are all goodness. The torments Jacob wrestled with were not physical. They were mental turmoils with an angel of darkness. Angels of darkness walk Earth just as angels of God's light do.

Contention of spiritual beliefs, greed, lusts, and sinful notions were dealt to Jacob in one long night. He wrestled with the powers of darkness. All angels of God watched Jacob struggle. This was more than a mental struggle. This was a fighting of good versus evil — a dark, fearful, grievous fight with wanton spirits of darkness all around. It would have been easy for him to surrender to what was offered him. This was a torment of the soul beyond imaginings. Angels of God surround the human and do not let the angels of darkness overtake any soul, but Jacob asked to fight these struggles by himself. God's angels did not interfere as he requested. Jacob proved to himself he was a man of strength, courage, and fortitude as he fought down the demons.

Over the years, with repeated storytelling, this legend changed from what happened and was written in a different way. The angel of darkness was defeated, as Jacob was inherently a man of God.

Why are angels of darkness here on Earth?

The angels of darkness are here on Earth by direction from the dark force. We do not write nor speak his name. These angels were sent to Earth to entice people to discover the wonders and eternal pleasures of hell: the pleasures of sex, gluttony, morbid entitlements — whatever the mind desires. These are wonders of extravagances, comforts, gratifications, delights, and amusements, as well as indulgences in the wicked and lowest senses.

The angels of darkness entice the soul to refute God and all his teachings and to follow the ways of darkness and gluttony. They take delight in any influences they can to seduce human minds. Any wars, any pains toward enemies, or any wicked thought brought into fruition delights them. This is not of God nor of ever-increasing bliss. We angels will ever fight against this. Let God into your soul. Lift your thoughts to God.

The forces of which you speak are as if this god of darkness is alive on Earth. This force enters the minds of the weak and those affected by unnatural substances. The angels of darkness whisper to people's minds just as God's holy angels do. These dark angels can cause lust, depravity, evilness, and hatred — things not perceived as goodness. The dark forces have no power when God's angels surround someone.

Angels of darkness whisper to the soul and mind to influence and work against God and God's plan for the world. The more the mind is influenced by these forces, the more it struggles against the ways of God.

People surrounded by angels of the darkness will be subject to performing acts of violence or acts not in the way of God.

God asked the angels of darkness to leave Earth, but they refused. They are waiting to overtake Earth. God will not allow the dark angels to own Earth. Angels of God are with all souls of Earth to lift their thoughts so that they do not dwell in the lowly level where the forces of evil, whose thoughts are sent on the lowest level of the mind, have influence. If you do not raise your quality of thought and you keep your mind in the lowest level, the angels of darkness can penetrate your mind.

They can lead you to commit acts that you normally would not consider. God's armies are continually battling these dark forces. You can ask the angels of God to surround you, and we will fight and protect the soul. Only when the soul requests entrance of the angels of darkness are they let in to influence the soul's mind. Let the angels of God always be with you. No evil can overtake you with our protection.

The angels of God will always prevail over the forces of darkness. The word of God is law. Many entities of God have powers that far outweigh any forces of evil. No one can stand against God or fight and win against him. God is above beings who stand against him.

Can the angels fight this evil?

Angelic warriors surround the targeted souls to protect them from evil. We angels of the Mallbon bring solace to wanting souls and lift souls to God. We are not the soldiers of God. We are the most holy angels of God, and we do his will. We protect our charges on Earth by the body and the soul. God's angel forces will fight and battle for goodness on this most lowly Earth. The world will be given whatever of God's forces that are needed.

How can we protect ourselves from these dark forces?

The gods of hell have powers to direct weakened minds. They will use these powers to seek and find human souls on Earth to try to make Earth their domain. There will be evilness in the air that is picked up by certain mental states of awareness. Drugs and alcohol may place the mind in a state vulnerable to these forces. If the mental level is low, this gives likened levels of darkness a way to penetrate thought. This can be done from the place known as hell. Making the mind strong and invulnerable will combat these forces. When evil or ignorance surrounds you, you will become as a beacon of light with all strength and power.

Hell is open for viewing from Earth, just as can be done from the heavens of God. The expectation of this is to one day inhabit Earth for the lower gods of other than the one holy God.

Earth is not a high world. It is most lowly in that needy souls are born here. This is a place to grow to God — or not grow and sink into despondency. Lift yourself up to be one who grows. Once you do this, teach others to become strong. The world needs many angels in and around it at all times to protect it from forces not of God. We want to keep the gods of darkness in another place and not let them loose upon Earth. Do not focus on them. Rather, think and feel love.

The God of Darkness

Can you describe the god of darkness?

The god of darkness appears as a human and has many angels of darkness around him. He emanates no aura and has no illumination. He gravitates to the depraved — the lower entities of the world — to entice them to his opulent world of hell. He offers them powers of creation to manifest anything they desire. This is a strong power.

The god of darkness can change his appearance; he can appear or disappear. You would not recognize him in a man's body. He can charm his prey through many methods. His demeanor is cunning, intelligent, well educated, and amusing. He has all the powers of the strongest gods. The god of darkness is without empathy, love, and compassion. He has strength and persistence. Should you feel his presence, ask your angels to protect you.

The god of darkness takes pleasure in havoc and disruptions on Earth. The movement of this god is most harmful to humankind. This most tremendous god rivals the god Jesus. The wickedness of this god is as strong as the love in God's realm. He wants Earth as his domain. When catastrophes occur, this is his time to bring people to his thinking. He meets those who desire power and greed to make his offers without their awareness of its happening. The people of Earth must fight against this god of darkness and stand up for the holy one, God in the heavens.

The spirits of dark force are not in the heavens at any time. Those in the heavens have no exposure to any forces pulling their souls to wickedness with the promise of all desires fulfilled. The souls of hell grow weary from creating with no hope of happiness. They may give a pretense of satisfaction, but there is no satisfaction. Hell is not a place one would want to enter or remain. God's heaven is one wonder after another, an essence of contentment with growth toward more and more love. No growth exists in the hells.

Dark spirits take many forms, all to deceive. Their power is manifested in ways not of the holy God of all in the heavens. Carnal satisfactions are repeated at will to bring the soul to the lowest, grossest levels of pleasure. They descend to morose levels where more crude and deviant actions envelop the soul — not in temporal ways, but forever. People on Earth cannot die and go to the hells. This cannot be done.

A world immersed in low thought cannot welcome God's light. The world needs many angels around it at all times to protect it from forces not of God.

Will the god of darkness ever be a politician or the leader of a country?

The force cannot live as a human through a life span. He can influence humans by enticing them with greed, avarice, and power. This will be done. This is a way to spread evilness in the world. This entity is leashed on Earth, but his gods of darkness remain in hell. He will not be a leader of countries but will try to influence people of power. If people could grow in their own strength and not be followers of these leaders of ignorance, this Earth would be a greater world.

Even if a person bespeaks of wealth and intelligence and is well read, well spoken, and well educated, he or she may still be subject to the will of this power. All should be aware of giving strength to other people who could be under the influence of this force. This dark force is cunning. It will take much to fight this evil.

War on Earth

Many will be lifted from Earth soon, as the wars escalate and illness reigns. The world must cease these horrific acts. This is not God's plan for humankind. Let now be the beginning of love on Earth.

As the Mideast wars, others plan ventures that are even more horrid.

Once people plan the demise of nations, the idea gains momentum and is difficult to change. We ache to help the suffering. We cluster near the war-torn souls to help, but we touch them only as a gentle breath. Angels feel more deeply than can be imagined. We feel the full range of emotions. We are, in a natural state, in bliss. We weep not, but we do feel empathy for the souls of Earth.

Our touch can bring peace to the soul if the soul is open to receiving it. A willing soul can meet us with thoughts of love, and all healing can penetrate the soul and body. Ask the angels to be with you now. Should a body be slain, pay this no heed, for the soul is alive through eternity! When wars come and bodies are slain, honor and praise them, for they are with God.

Do not turn away from honor or from defending your family or fellow citizens. This is not given as a way of life; however, war dictates the path of the warrior. This Earth is not a utopia. People must uphold what they know in their hearts is right. This is not to say that souls are not to forgive and bless the attacker. This is to say to give to the world what belongs to the world, and give to God what belongs to God.

The Chelton Soldiers in the heavens achieved this balance. They are God's soldiers who fight and bless their enemies that they may find their way. They hold the highest and most honorable qualities and overtake all enemies of God and of the heavens. At the same time, they send love and compassion to their enemies. They hold no hatred in their hearts. The realization that battle is necessary gives them courage to fight. They have awareness of their enemies' consciousness and respect the motions of war.

One on Earth may not understand the full significance of what I'm describing. The Chelton Soldiers in the heavens are not men of war. They are men of extreme wisdom, fortitude, value, and honor in any circumstance. These are angels of the strongest morality and the highest dedication to God. They are at the ready to serve God in any capacity. They know the movements of any beings against the one God. They will not let any force against God enter the heavenly realm. No force can penetrate their defenses. Soldiers bear not only the honor of serving God but also hold extreme compassion and love for even their enemies. This is the level to which they have grown in the heart. These are souls of honor and wisdom. All angels look at them lovingly.

People of Earth fight with hate in their hearts and with greed and bitterness in their minds. This is not to be indulged. People of Earth: You need not be filled with hate. If the souls understood the human feelings of their enemies, the enemies would cease to exist, for all souls of Earth are alike in the ways of the soul. Put the effort instead into bettering yourself, to being the most wonderful person you can be. Give no attention to harming others, for violence only begets violence.

Must you experience the horrors of war to know it's not the correct way? Because a soldier is courageous and kills without feeling, do not think you can become a soldier in the heavens. The angels are chosen by God. God knows the love in their hearts and the feelings of their souls. The movements of humans must evolve before you can attain the status of an angel. This may take multitudes of lifetimes to achieve. Love and kindness must encompass Earth.

Malevolent Practices

If a person curses God, will he or she be punished?

If you curse God because of something you feel is unfair in your life, God understands these feelings. A soul will not perish because of confusion or ignorance. The soul may utter words of disgust for God and the heavens without repercussion. This is normal for the souls of Earth.

When you are in a crisis in your life and have battled all ways to live, you might curse God for not helping you. God knows the words are from frustration and fear. God is merciful and sends angels in times of great need.

How do terrorists fit into God's plan?

They have a religion. When spirituality is reduced to outward rituals of conformity with no depth of feeling, frustration has no release but hatred and violence. No light of God can enter the soul. You must open your heart to God to feel the heart of the soul. You must feel the transformation of the soul within rather than the outward power over others.

Will peace ever come to Earth?

When the light of God radiates on Earth, worlds shall watch in awe because wonders will occur. Knowledge will replace ignorance. Kindness will replace the crudeness. The world will glow from the wonder arising over the world of Earth. All shall rejoice and give thanks to God for his works. Angels will wander the Earth to give loving thoughts to all. This wonder can bring the world to joys not experienced in the history of Earth. Not only will this occur in the physical, but also in the spiritual state. This level will begin to be perceived. People will think they have extraordinary powers, but the spirit will be visible to all on Earth.

People must begin anew as they must know the reversal of intentions on Earth is of extreme necessity. Religions are not simple systems of belief. It is the method in which you live life. Let your religion be the celebration of the joy of the self. Live life to help others with their lives. Radiate kindness and love.

The soul is not to be in sour penance. The soul is to exalt, to dance in freedom, and to shine on Earth as a Child of God. Many are now mentioning the fear of God in religion. There should be no fear of God, for he is all blessings to all souls. Religion is not to bind the soul from expression any longer. It is to free the soul in the celebration of life and the glories of God.

Can we try to attain psychic powers?

Concerning powers of the psychic — as voices, visions, communications with ghosts, and any powers attained through delusions, incantations, or unnatural substances — these are not to be sought. Should you be approached by apparitions in this life, they are to be ignored and refuted, for they will only distract you from your true path. Psychic powers will not come from the encouragement of these methods. These true powers can only be discerned by the growth to God. Should you feel you have derived powers from other sources, you will discover you are self-deluding.

Be most careful of taking on beliefs unless verified by you personally. The verification may come through dreams or from angels. Be careful not to induce demons through invocation or writing spells that are not of God or of the angels. Do not try to invoke magic. People are ignorant of forces outside of Earth. The creation of bringing evil forces forward is not to be practiced. This could harm all on Earth.

The souls are God's children, not souls of another force. You can gain what humans consider to be supernatural powers through devotion to God. Any powers received other than from God are self-deception. This is a warning to people of Earth not to proceed with the black arts. This is so important.

Is there anything else you want to include about evil?

Yes. The being named Satan is not a god of darkness. This is a name conjured by humans to weld ignorance and evilness into a specific name. Neither omen nor signal is to be used to invoke this evilness. This is not to be practiced.

CHAPTER THREE

The God

We will now provide the most powerful words ever given to any mortal. These words are sacred.

As the soul asks, "Is God alive?" this God is with the soul in all actuality, all power, all love, and all energy. This soul is also with all other souls on all worlds, in all space, and in all universes. The one God is all-pervading, all love, all energy, and all-knowing. This God is more than a mortal can conceive. God is all that is and all that ever will be.

If you create a picture of God in the mind, you will see a man of wisdom and of love. This is only a part of God, for he surpasses any concept of what people can envision. God directs the holy angels in a multitude of ways. We answer only to God. God is intensity. He is mass. God is energy beyond description. He appears as a man but is immersed in light of his own making. God existed always. There will never be an end or a beginning to God.

You Will Meet God

Will I see God and the heavens after this life?

When a soul gains entrance to see God, the ecstasy is beyond description. Forever a soul yearns to be nearer to God, to feel the love again. Many lives, many deaths, and many experiences will be sought by the souls to grow closer to the one God of all.

You place yourself in the heavens but yearn for a celestial passage to be nearer to God. At the end of your life, after the last breath is taken, the angels adorn you and usher you to meet the God. This may seem like a moment or a thousand moments, for time is not used.

It will seem to you that no other souls exist except you and God. No other communication will shake you to the depths of your soul as this meeting. You will view and speak with the God of all gods. This is more blissful, more terrifying, and more real than anything known. You will shake in the soul. You will gasp and cry tears of joy. No soul can stand before God in all courage without folding in honor to the immensity of feelings.

Even a breath of God lifts the soul to more depth of feeling than can be expressed. A word from God brings awe to the receiver. A touch from God envelopes the soul in more bliss than is bearable. These words are to be honored as truth. We angels give the truth now to the souls of Earth.

At the lifting of the soul, all will be made clear, and the soul will know of God's love. Angels will cradle the soul as it's lifted to the heavens. One day, you will know of this. As you become aware of God's mercy, love, and blessings, you will honor God in all thought.

The lifting of souls is as caressing the soul into the loving arms of angels. When this occurs, the soul cherishes the feelings. A soul asks questions of the angels, and all is answered through thought. As the soul lifts through levels to see the heavens, the experiences become softer, finer, and more and more blissful.

A soul is assured to meet God. The soul may then speak with God, and God will answer. This is an honor and a feeling only the soul can fathom. The feeling that envelops in God's presence is with the soul through eternity. No soul can meet God without trembling, falling on the knees, or knowing the ultimate fulfillment of all desires. This is the greatest experience a soul can know.

Are there more significant feelings than knowing that you will now meet God?

The realms of the heavens are each more blissful than the last. Once the soul has seen the heavens, it is ushered to the openings of the heavens where it assimilates all that has occurred.

All questions of the soul are answered to the soul's satisfaction. All is understood in completion. One may view past lives in order to prepare for future endeavors. Angels prepare and adorn the soul to meet God.

When one is brought before God, more humility and more graciousness than the soul has ever known is brought forth. A soul begs God for mercy only to find God is all mercy. A soul desires love from the God more than any other feeling only to find God is all love.

How is it to meet God after this life?

The meeting is only between the soul and the Almighty God. No heavenly creature is audience to the meeting. No words on Earth can prepare you for meeting the one God. The most that anyone can feel is expressed before God. With every word, every breath, and every motion, the heart is in the most bliss you can feel. No words of Earth can explain this, for it is expression beyond comprehension.

When meeting God, ecstasy thunders through the soul with such force that the spirit will shake in exhilaration. Nothing, no experience, not all lives, nor all deaths can equal this feeling. This is love beyond explanation. All is given in this exchange. All love is known.

The angels are motioned to bring the soul to its resting place. At this interjection, the soul places itself in a heaven where it feels the most comfort. This will be near others of the same growth level as the soul.

All That Is

Who is God, and what is God's purpose?

God, as you choose to call him, is a being in the seat of the highest heaven who directs all movement of all that exists. God is a wonder unto all worlds, all heavens, all space, and all existence. The one God of all intelligence is alive in the heavens. God is all love, all wisdom and all energy — all that is in all spectrums.

All creation is from this wisdom. All existence in the heavens in all places and in all space and time have God's imprint. The word of God is all-powerful. All is everything. Thought functions in worlds not only with material things but with all substance — all ethereality, all form, and all matter in all strata. God interprets feelings as the language of all entities.

God is a name for an indescribable being. He is the absolute perfection, the all-consuming love, the energy, the powerfulness, the intelligence, and the organization of the one God of all gods and of all existence. It is more than you can understand. The heavens are beyond explanation. All perfection, all life, emanates from this being: the life in all worlds, in all strata — all is love beginning with God's thought. No other being exists equating the intelligence, the love, and the complexities of the one holy God of all gods and all that exists.

How does God appear?

God is all spirit and light. The Almighty God is as a man, but breath and words cannot describe him. He is masculine. He is as a spirit or as a flesh-and-blood man. He is in light and love generated by him. He is all-knowledgeable in all attributes.

God appears to us as emanating light and love, as does the Holy Spirit. He is comprised of an immense intensity of feelings. God is not approachable, even by the Men of the Mallbon, unless it's requested. If an audience is granted, God is approachable and appears as a pleasing man. God is the most sacred of all beings and is surrounded by his emanations of light. The light encompasses feelings even an angel of God cannot explain. This God of all gods is with all love.

God gives an impression of being only with you and immersed in you, but he is with worlds unending and entities unknown at the same time. He appears as an intense power — light, love, and energy. Gods and archangels surround him. The majesty and glory of the one great God is beyond description. The perfection is immeasurable. The holiness, the powerfulness, and the eternal wisdom he encompasses are in all truth.

God lifts all minds. God brings love to all hearts. God loves all on Earth more deeply than can be conceived. The soul is free to move toward God or away from him. The soul may embrace God or deny him. People have known of God from the beginning yet have fought against giving themselves to God. You can not only lift to God but also choose to grow enormously in this life.

What would you do or say if God stood before you this moment? Can you speak and behave as if God were with you? God *is* with you. God knows every thought, every feeling, and every action — everything. God issued your birth on Earth so that you might grow into enlightenment or grow to the elevation of the spirit. All are welcomed in the heavens, which is God's abode. God loves and blesses all souls unconditionally.

These are not empty words. God adores your freedom of choice.

God gave you this. God smiles at your individualism. Should a moment happen in your life whereby you could hold the love God has for you, the soul could not accept the bliss. The acceptance of God and angelic figures is to be from a perspective of not seeing and not hearing them because behaviors would be affected.

The Voice of God

Have the angels heard God's voice? Can you describe it?

The one God of all gods need not speak or move. He feels, and all feelings emanate from him. The finest, most intricate thought put forth is from the one God. This is irrefutable. No thought is sent forth from God that is not of the most high. If a thought is engaged, it's a law and is enacted through the heavens.

The voice of God has been heard in the heavens. The voice is calm, deep, and strong. It can be used to speak with those who do not understand thought.

The majesty and glory of the one great God is beyond description. His perfection is immeasurable. The holiness, the powerfulness, and the eternal wisdom he encompasses is in all truth.

Gods in the Heavens

How do we address a god in the heavens?

This is not a prayer. Prayers are to be directed to God or to Jesus, who keeps watch over Earth. When addressing a god or an angel, give your most humble and sincere appearance. Give homage in benevolent thought so that he might listen and understand why he was called to you.

This is a great honor to any human. Prepare your words now to ask, should this magnificent opportunity arise. Meet the god with a gasp of thankfulness. The honor bestowed on you is one of greatness. Should it be a moment, don't waste a second with thoughts of material desires.

Call to a god only in the direst circumstances or to enact a desire for humankind, not for selfish wants. Give great and strong thought before summoning a god of the heavens or an angel of the one God in heaven. A god directs multitudes of humans. The angels oversee all on Earth. Is your desire worthy of their presence? We have the world's destiny in our hands.

Each god has varied strengths or areas with which each seeks to help. If a particular way is requested, one may try to communicate with the gods themselves. Each person, angel, or god need not be on Earth to communicate. A strong thought may be carried and delivered anywhere.

Ask to speak to a god through the strongest thought that you can produce. Some gods will only respond to thought, not to words, as they are on the finer levels. Some gods will respond neither to words nor thought from low entities such as souls of Earth. Ask with a deeply humble, not haughty, heart with the strongest, most sincere, loving thought, and beg that the god answers. In this way, a god in the heavens may enter your abode and speak to you.

If you cannot see him or her, the thought will still be received. The thought may be received on a subconscious level. Either is valid and is in your consciousness. This is not to be done frivolously. This is to be asked in the most sacred and sincere communication.

The prayer to the one God above all other gods should be asked in even more sacred and sincere thought. Rest assured, the prayer to the one God is received. Angels are given the requests as God's holy messengers of the souls of Earth.

The Soul Leads the Way

Is there a specific way to reach God?

The moment you realize you belong to God and not merely to yourself, your demeanor changes. You will now walk toward God. The soul can stray no more. The soul will walk each day with God in heart and mind. To move away from God is inconceivable.

Now the purpose is known, the future revealed. Let this be known to all or to any. No one can pull away now, for the way to God is found. The path is clear and unfettered. The soul has found the light and cannot veer from the way. It is as a moth to a flame.

Understandings unfold before you as if they were known all along. Once God is sought, desires of Earth seem fruitless and fall away. Now, as the soul has felt even a faint glimpse of God, all belongings crumble and fade in importance. The ways of Earth are meaningless because eternity glistens. Problems of life become nonexistent because the soul now knows of heaven. This life can now be enjoyed as never before.

The fleeting life will be seen as a journey of the soul. Circumstances of this life are viewed as a dream, to fade as the light emerges to brighten all things. The moment is joyful because it's no longer serious; it's a moment of play. As the soul lives this life, it is affected less and less by the ways of humanity. The mind and heart of the soul strengthens as it moves closer to God.

A person of severity and seriousness can be lighthearted, for this person now knows the way to God has been opened. There exist in the life no insecurities, no wrongdoings, and no indecisions. You have found your soul, and the soul has found its way to God. The soul leads the way. The soul lives on through eternity and is always protected. People ever seek happiness through the physical. Yet once the soul is opened to feel, the path to God is known. More true happiness than has ever been experienced is now felt.

Action is necessary as the earthly life is a physical life. Movements of actions are not the way to fulfillment but are to be indulged in joyously. God gave you physical bodies to use and enjoy. Work is a part of this. Labors are a part of the earthly life. The movements of the body are unique in many worlds. Take joy in the physical.

All parts of life are temporal effects and are to be experienced to bring you to God. A life is to be lived to the fullest through the mind, the body, the heart — all. The ways to God are many, and many doors are open to reach God. If you hold welcoming love for humanity in your heart, this will guide you to God.

People tend to feel the religion they personally hold is the only true way to God and that no other belief system is correct. Even if your soul keeps no more than goodness in your heart, it is the correct path. A soul needs only to talk to God to know God is with it. The soul of each person lifts to express to God in its own way. The loving God will mend all ills and make plans for all the world.

What is my path?

The moment you find a path to God, all manner of change befalls you. No longer are you wallowing in misdirection, even though the path might be wrought with inaccuracies. The goal is to bring the soul closer to God. Find a way comfortable for your soul.

If you question and feel uneasy about the teachings, that particular method might not be the correct way. Many ways lead to God. Many may follow Jesus, as he has dominion over Earth. This is a wonderful path — but not the only path.

One day, all will find God. One day, each will see God. Alter the life to encompass God. Nothing is without God at any time. The developments of humankind are of many levels of growth. A soul will gravitate to where it feels most comfortable. The mind is ever seeking happiness.

The soul knows the truth of all things. Unless one can integrate these, the mind remains in ignorance. You are to hold yourself in high esteem and give reverence to the one God in the heavens. Give no one dominion over you, for only God holds this dominion. A mind of weakness and of disassembly cannot work wonders in the life. A mind disheartened or despondent is in stagnation of low thought. No angel can penetrate a closed soul. No longer are you to think yourself as a lowly or unworthy creature. Open to God and be a being of all possibilities. Immerse in all life.

Every Soul Returns to God

Will God punish us in heaven?

Some people may seek God through religions. Many believe punishment after death is now factual. It is not. God will be sought after the death of the body. God gives no punishment to the soul at any time. He works through the mind and heart of the soul to help the soul realize the growth needed.

Each level of the multitudes of the heavens reflects a level of soul growth. The higher levels are closer to the God and filled with more and more bliss. The soul, after the death of the body and after meeting with God, places itself in a heaven where it feels most comfortable. The soul needs a physical body on Earth and in the lower worlds in order to grow to God through the senses.

After each life, the soul will return to God. Not one soul is given to the hells. All find solace in the heavens. In the loving heavens, a soul who has committed sins on humankind will find the contemplative redirection needed. Each soul will desire to be closer to God but will stay where it alone feels deserving of its merits. The one God looks at each soul, knowing all growth and all that is needed for the consciousness to grow.

God is only love. No anger exists. No fear is to be held, for God dispenses only direct love. The image of God reflects no specific race. God is an emanation of energy. The face of God, if seen, can profess no specific race. Each soul sees what it desires in the face of God. The intensity of light from God and from the Holy Spirit is beyond what the eye can perceive.

You Cannot Separate from God

God knows everything occurring on Earth. God is in heaven and is also with you this very moment. One day, you will understand this. The one God is not to be viewed on Earth, only his emissaries. Angels deliver God's word on Earth. No people are to say they have viewed God, for they have not. No people can say they have heard the voice of God, for they have heard the voice of an angel.

Though God appears to no humans on Earth, he knows every second of your life. He knows every thought in your mind and every movement in your heart. God knows all souls and loves all souls in ways not understood by humanity.

You are part of God. You cannot separate yourself from God, as the soul of each self is God's. As a person on Earth, you might think you are alone to do whatever you want, but you must be aware that every movement has covenants to abide. These are known in the soul and mind. One day, you will know God. You will experience God not as a separate entity but as a part of you. We wish that we could explain this, but it doesn't seem possible.

God gave you this world to make of it what you will. Spend not one moment in self-indulgence but give thanks for all the blessings. We angels wish the world more happiness than we can express. It need not move in a backward development. This world can move forward in the growth to love. One reason God brought souls to Earth was to let them breathe in a human body. The souls were needy, and this world was given to them so that they could come together in harmony not only to exist on it but also to enhance it.

Create as if in God's Presence

Is God here?

Bring the name of God into the world. This is not a name used only by the religious. God is not so far above Earth that he can't be received. God is here, now, alive. God is with you this moment. You may pray to him, talk to him, and feel him. If his light is beyond the spectrum of your eyes or the sound is beyond what your ears can hear, know God and God's angels are always with you.

Make your life as if God were in your presence, for he is with you. Create in your earthly ways to bring wondrous ideas into implementation. Design your life to move in the ways that you dream. This is a life force given by God. Don't be content just to exist and not explore new horizons. Treasure this life. Bring your most precious soul to the world. Give no pretense, no masking of emotion. Give neither platitudes nor movements of placid repetitions. Leave your mark on the world. Give something of value to humanity.

Creation does not end but expands into more and better. So it is with each soul as each grows in wonderment. A word from God breathes life into particles of energy. Dare to imagine the creations before you in worlds yet unknown. God is always building, creating, moving, and generating. Be part of this energy.

As the most holy being moves through the heavens and all worlds, a life on Earth does not seem of much importance, but this is not so. Every soul in every place is of tremendous worth. When the end of your life takes form, you will know your life and your soul mattered in God's design. Each soul is most cherished. All particles in all existence belong to God. God created all things, all space, all light, and all sound. You are a part of this. No one who dwells on Earth is nearer to God than you are at this moment.

CHAPTER FOUR

The Goddess and Other Extensions of God

There was a time, hundreds of thousands of lifetimes to measure, when God chose the female goddess to reign as a loving mother of his child. Ameragyn is the hallowed Mother of the god Jesus. She is the Goddess of Obon and the sacred Mother of the Sons of God. God chose her to bring forth sons in the heavens. A goddess of intense beauty and wisdom was asked whether she might carry the Children of God. This was not only in spirit but in the physical as well.

The goddess was all beauty and all feeling. She was all feminine. She is the goddess now known as the mate of God in the ways of heaven, which is different from the descriptions you've been given on Earth. The Goddess exists in many worlds in the heavens and throughout all existence. She illuminates. She holds the honors of all spectrums in all worlds. She breathes life into the Children of God.

A son was born to God from the union between the God and the Goddess. He grew most powerful. He asked God for all power over all worlds. This was denied. He turned against God, as he felt he had all the powers of God. He became as a force of darkness for all time. God will not avenge his son nor will he avenge works on Earth that are not of his dictates. God loves as a human cannot comprehend. The love God holds for his sons is unequaled.

God created another soul and his merging with the Goddess created the body of Christ in the heavens. This is true. The Goddess carried the child Jesus just as Mary carried the child on Earth. A child born in the heavens of light and love is a blessed god. This soul was given the name of Relelemet and is also known as Jesus.

All in the heavens rejoiced at Jesus's holy birth. All exist in eternity, and the souls in the celestial heavens are as love personified. The cherished son exists in the heavens for all time. All love permeates the heavens. This soul was created by God to become a god from birth.

Jesus grew to become a god of greatness. He honors God, the Father in heaven, and the parents he was given on Earth. He asked to overlook Earth and the world of Liloh. This was given to him.

What is this world you mentioned called Liloh?

This is a world of exalted souls. People of this world can be in a human body or in spirit form. This world is beyond perfection. No mortal world can surpass the beauty of this world. The beauty is almost as a heaven. This is a world of immense vegetation. It's now a world of the higher souls who abide on Earth.

The people of the world of Liloh bring joy to all minds. They use telepathy rather than speech. They know each other's thoughts and communicate with all beings in this manner. This is a world with many similarities to Earth. The people of the world of Liloh come to Earth to help in times of extreme danger. No warring exists on Liloh, for they are an amiable people.

Many races of humans and many species of animals subsist on this world. This is not a place of remoteness as Earth is. Beings of Liloh communicate with those of other worlds. A higher form of lawfulness and cooperation exists there.

Jesus

When you envision God and the Children of God, you might imagine a man on a throne with all his sons about him. This is what the people of Earth picture. This vision is in error, as God is perceived as a figure of all light. The Holy Spirit, Abraham, and Jesus are all perceived as light. Imagine the illumination!

Jesus is a god in the heavens. God, the Father in heaven, gives this god, Jesus, dominion over Earth and other worlds. He is a god of great worth, as he sits on the right hand of God and God asks him to meet with the human souls. This god is of wonderful ways. The people of Earth refer to him as the Son of God. This is a reality not only on Earth but also in heaven. Jesus is the god of being in the flesh. The souls of Earth follow him.

Jesus is the world's savior in that he appeared on Earth to all souls to let it be known that the body and soul are one. This means the soul, when lifted to the heavens, becomes as a body with the density of flesh — if this is desired.

The god Jesus is the true Son of God. He is a most revered god in that he is powerful in many ways. He hears and responds to prayers. He appears to many on Earth. This most hallowed god will again appear to humankind. He loves the children of Earth. This is a god most sacred, as he feels all humans' pain, all emotions of all prayers, all sadness, and all despondency. He has encompassed all of humanity's ignorance to help lift souls toward God.

The holy ways of Jesus are sacred in God's eyes. He is a god who absolves people's sins and misgivings. Jesus has great compassion, love, and mentions of worth for those of Earth. The holiness of this god is that he only sees the goodness in human beings. He dispenses miraculous work on Earth. To forgive all sins, forgive all obscenities, and pardon all transgressions is the gift of this great and sacred god.

Jesus can take the pain from humankind to free them to sin no more. Jesus lifts souls to God who are so immersed in sinfulness that they cannot see God. They are given pardons for all works against God. Imagine the mercifulness of the god Jesus!

Speak to Jesus in a most humble way. This god stands with you at trials of defense, speaking of your love and your worthiness to lift to the higher heavens. Jesus in heaven lifts us from wars and pain, from hurt and sorrow. This is what you ask for. Jesus hears these pleas and helps in ways unknown to you.

The holy ways of Jesus are sacred in God's eyes. Jesus is a great and glorious god in the highest realm. Jesus will speak your name to abide in these heavens. Not all on Earth will give credence to these words, but these are truth.

Abraham

Is Jesus God's only son?

You will now see the truth as we tell the story. God created three sons. One is Abraham, one is Relelemet (Jesus), and one is of the dark force. The most wonderful delight came with the creation of the first son, Abraham. Abraham is an entity of pure light, not in a physical body. He grew as a powerful god, not without the powers of God. He grew into the god he will forever be. He began as a thought of God who willed him into existence.

Abraham will always be all goodness and all light. He was created of energy and light yet he appears, hears, sees, speaks, and feels as a man. He does not consider that he is the Son of God but rather an entity of light, not unlike the Holy Spirit. Abraham is a most sacred god of the heavens. No force that is not of God may go against him, for he diminishes all of evilness or little worth. This god only need think a thought and it's done as he deems. He is almighty in the dispensing of justice.

Abraham is all magnificence, all light, all power, all volume, and all holy. He was created of the same brilliance as the Holy Spirit of the most sacred energies. He appears as a man immersed in light and color in sacredness and benevolence. This god is with all gods in the heavens and overlooks all God's creations. His power is beyond explanation. His eminence is brilliant beyond imagination.

This most sacred god sits with the God and holds to his every thought and expression. This god sits on the left hand of God, the Father in heaven. He is strength and courage, all-knowing and all-seeing.

This god is not shown to humans but works in unseen ways. All ways not of God, all creatures working against God, and all evilness on Earth will meet this god. When you encounter evilness, ask this god in heaven for protection and courage against this force. This god will send angels to you, for he is aware of even the smallest and lowest of forces against God. When a force that is not of god is free on Earth, Abraham and the soldiers of the heavenly realms will combat them. This is assured by God.

All ways that are not of God will cease to exist for a time because of this great god. This god will let God's way prevail on Earth. Seek Abraham in all courage and honor, all standing for the ways of God. People of Earth stand with this god in the heavens, for he is most honored and most sacred.

The Holy Spirit

What is the Trinity?

The Trinity — the Father, the Son, and the Holy Spirit — are a fact when looked at from the perspective of Earth. So much more exists than from this limited view. God the Father, the Mother, Jesus, and the Holy Spirit exist not only in the heart but in all places.

"Trinity" is a word made by humans to describe God, the Son of God, and the Holy Spirit. This is a simplified version from one perspective only. Ameragyn is the female who merged with God to beget Jesus. Mary was the female who bore him on Earth, for he was born in the heavens and on Earth.

Is the Holy Spirit equal to God?

They are as one. Only the God in the heavens is over the people of Earth. The Holy Spirit is of another purpose. This is the emanated love throughout all. This spirit is not concerned with God's organizations. This spirit and the one God are all feeling. They are different in the reasons for existence. This is difficult for us to explain in your understanding. The feelings in the heavens are intense and pure, unencumbered as they are on Earth. The bliss in the heavens emanates from the one God and the Holy Spirit. Love beyond comprehension, sent to all creatures, all worlds, all existence, emanates from this one Holy Spirit. Without this, all love in all existence would cease to be.

The existence will always be and will never cease. All structures of all life are built solely on this holy love. The purposes go far beyond this explanation. This is an incomprehensible, purposeful emanation in the heavens, structuring all growth and all mentions of creation in all strata.

Who is the Holy Spirit?

God is in the image of an actual, particular human, whereas the Holy Spirit cannot be seen. He emits light so far-reaching and intensely brilliant that only the form can be viewed. He is a part of God because they are one and the same, yet each is a particular entity. God is a concrete figure. The Holy Spirit is only in spirit. It will not ever be definite. It will remain a spirit eternally. One cannot speak the name of the Holy Spirit. This shall not be given to the people of Earth.

We can send thought to this spirit, but we cannot speak aloud. The infusion is of the finest, most intricate level imaginable. Let us explain: If one shouts loudly, this is the most heavy, gross level. If one speaks, it's a slightly finer level. If one whispers, it's even finer. If one sends thought, it's a finer level still. If one radiates, this is even higher and lighter. The Holy Spirit is the most tender, lightest, and finest of all expressions.

You may not speak to the Holy Spirit except through angels. We ask the archangels to intervene. We bow and tremble before its mightiness. We don't fear it, for it is all love. We humble before this greatest of gods. The spirit in God and humankind's image exists on the world of the celestial. This God is of the highest and is part of the one God. It is most holy in all ways.

We cannot see the Holy Spirit. It isn't visible even to us. The light and power from this spirit is not conceivable. The feelings sent by the spirit are so profound and intense that we cannot even approach this. We tremble near this power. The love is radiated throughout all worlds in existence. We cannot speak with the spirit of all light and will not approach this spirit. The intensity of love is overwhelming, even to us. We honor this spirit and kneel to this power.

The power of the Holy Spirit is masculine. The souls, the gods, the angels, and the archangels are all in God's image. This is the shape you know as a human. The spirit of light and power is in the shape of a human and radiates emanations of intense love.

The Hierarchy of Heaven

What is the organizational succession in the heavens?

- God
- the Holy Spirit
- Ameragyn
- Jesus
- Abraham

- Melecite
- all the gods in the heavens, (such asAlhelphelian)
- all the archangels
- the Men of the Mallbon
- all the angels of varied levels
    - the angel's appointees:
    - the Women of Question
    - the Men of Old
    - the Men of Decision
    - the Men of One
    - the souls of the celestial heavens
    - the souls of the highest worlds

Who is Melecite?

Melecite is a most sacred god of the worlds of people growing toward God. This is a god of the most sacred thoughts. This god humbles before God and speaks only in thought. This god is gentle, loving, and pure in thought and action.

Tears may form in the eyes of this god at the loving ways performed by humankind. This god is truly sacred in all ways. He is a god of more compassion than humankind can understand. The souls of humanity beg to be in his presence. He answers souls with tears of love. If this god touches your soul, you fall on your knees to feel the love he presents. More tenderness than one has ever felt can be experienced at his touch.

Many on Earth cannot experience the intensity of this. His touch is given slowly because the soul of man is not developed enough to feel the emotions it may bring. He opens the emotions to feel love beyond words. This is a life-changing emotion. The soul is open, responding, and vulnerable to all life. If this is experienced, even for a second, you will beg to feel it again. This god is sacred in all ways.

If people reach the highest heaven, can they be appointed as angels or gods?

This is not to be coveted. God alone chooses these appointments. Not every soul wants to achieve these appointments. There are many ways to exist to fulfill the soul in completion. This can be done, but it is not likely because Earth is the lowest of all worlds and holds the souls of the most needy. The souls must go through many births and deaths, many experiences, and many feelings. It must grow in the soul to one most holy.

God watches the growth of all souls, and he alone appoints angels to their designated status. A soul of Earth may aspire to evolve the soul to the highest. We do not mean to say this cannot be done, as wonders do occur.

Angels are of many growth levels as well as diverse applications and interests. The Mallbon angels are the realm of angels overlooking Earth. God chose us to become angels of the Mallbon because this suited our specialties. We chose to help those in need. People of Earth are the souls of the most need. If you have an intense desire to become an angel, ask God. The needed qualities will be opened to you.

Alhelphelian

We ask for the wisdom of the great god Alhelphelian. This is a god of justice in all worlds. The laws governing all worlds and all universes are the same. All laws are necessary for the worlds to function smoothly.

Freedom is a gift to be cherished, but laws help enact the freedoms. Freedom without any rules will result in chaos. The laws guide souls to right action. No punishment occurs for the incoherence of the laws. The laws are meant to show the way that many souls can survive together in harmony. The way the world sees this is to rebel against them. It seems the most important laws are meant to protect all from the few.

This god will sit in judgment against the few who choose not to live in harmony. They will know all the ways of God. They will know and understand the purpose of each law in the universes.

- Love God and the creatures of God in the highest.
- Be the highest soul you are capable of being. Put on no airs. Be as you are.
- Give love to all entities of God. Give love to all souls you encounter. Understand them and lift them to a more glorious life, if it is possible.
- Let the movement of creation flow generously through your soul. Give the movement of creation to all you encounter.
- Hurt not one being of God. God's creations serve him. Understand them. Do nothing to harm them in physical or mental ways. Let all live in God's splendor.

- No malice, no condemnation, and no distrust may occur. On Earth, these do occur. Love is inhibiting the dissention of these distrustful feelings on a few of the lower worlds.
- No gods are before the greatest God in the heavens. All other gods are under this God.
- The mother and father you have chosen are to be honored in the highest. Give love and honor to these earthly parents.

The god Alhelphelian is not a god of mercy, yet he does not punish. Each soul will make amends for individual actions if it's warranted. This god will oversee to note whether justice needs to be dispersed. Much is dismissed with laughter, as gods of justice have great humor. The more learned seem so error-free that any deviations are quickly observed. Other souls rush in to help in whatever way is needed.

The Men of One answer to this god and are directed by him. They act as a jury of your peers would act. These are learned men in varied ways who have complete understanding of human frailties. They discuss and determine all deviations from the normal growth of the soul.

This overlooking god is a welcome sight to all, as he is strong and powerful but also gentle and compassionate. Direct movements against God are not tolerated, and this god will stand firm to protect the heavens from the disciples of evilness. This god alone knows the disciples of the evil gods. This is one way to depart any evilness trying to infiltrate the heavens or do harm to God or God's followers. Alhelphelian is a god in the heavens protecting the worlds of God and the heavens of God.

Love in other worlds will always exist. Nothing will ever permeate these worlds with evilness. We angels attest to this. We are truly the angels of God, the Father in the heavens, and we stand by his direction.

Gods versus Archangels

What's the difference between a god and an archangel?

The gods, luminous and in all magnificence, are huge in appearance. The stature and powerfulness is tremendous. The brightness emanating from these gods is beyond comprehension. The gods are what you would consider gigantic from the human perspective. The gods are almost too brilliant for the eyes of humans to see and comprehend.

The archangels are angels lifted to the movement of God's actions. They are not gods who are always in God's presence, but they rule over worlds in God's universes. Gods oversee varied ways and workings. Gods are given charge of all things, whereas archangels are charged with watching over multitudes of God's angelic forces.

Archangels appear larger than the normal height of humans on Earth. They are in luminosity, in the glow of God's light, in warmth, and in all love. Gods are in laughter and in joyousness. They are light-hearted and give great wonder to words and thoughts. All are absolute perfection, all magnificence, and all bliss. The gods are with the one God and adore him.

Are we to pray only to God, or can we pray to these lesser gods?

Pray not to these gods but to the one God, the Almighty Father in heaven. When you pray to God, all the gods hear your prayers. One day, you will see these gods in the heavens.

Gods reside over all that is affecting life. Gods are rulers of every force in all worlds. Make no mistake, these gods are with the one God in the heavens and answer only to him. There are gods upon gods in the heavens. Each is more powerful and loving than the next. Gods are architects of the worlds and all within the worlds. Gods rule over all aspects in the heavens and on all worlds. They number in the multitudes. The gods are always creating and balancing. People should strive to be as a god.

CHAPTER FIVE

Creation

Can you explain the creation of the world?

Creation began as a word from God. God created Earth through the movement of energy swirling into form. In other words, the foliage, the seas, and the mountains all came into being. The outer Earth was a heaven. The gods were about, creating under God's direction. Many species of life matured and died out before the entrance of humanity. The formation was not as other worlds with all perfection. The world of Earth was a reflection of human consciousness. Earth was created for people to inhabit and grow in all ways.

This is the lowest world. People must be able to exist on Earth before moving on to higher worlds. This means to coexist with other species and other races. Earth's creation was designed to supply all materials needed to support humankind as physical beings. The world is a wonder from God. People can use it as a wonder, or they can destroy it. This world is your gift from God to do with as you wish.

Can you tell us about the creation of humanity?

Beyond imaginable time, the human being was created. The heavens were divided into spheres for the multitudes of souls. People are assigned specific tasks, individually and in groups. The organization in the heavens is all perfection. The purpose of the physical human is to house the soul so that it may grow through the senses without seeing or hearing God. Earth is a much older place than the people of Earth believe.

The beings first brought to Earth were from other worlds. They were appointed by God. They requested to be explorers of the new world. These were the greatest of souls, men and women of nine races of humankind. These begot the varied races of people on Earth. Over time, the people mixed to enact many cultures. They were able to move into separate areas of the world over much time to develop their own character traits. It took many eons to develop the varied characteristics and languages.

The hardships of life wore on these great souls, and the humans developed frailties as the generations grew. This was a lower world in more ways than they had ever known. The world was harsh with new movements. It was difficult to survive in the body. The world became more difficult to live in, and humanity withered into a lesser species.

People must rise now to their intended worth. The time is now. There has been little growth for a very long time. People have not progressed except in small ways.

How did the different races of humanity come about?

Many races and cultures exist not only on Earth but also on all worlds. As Earth progresses into space travels, humankind will know of the races of beings not known on this world. All beings in all strata are Children of God. All are in the image of God. The different races are evolved because of specific environs that have endured over time.

The purpose is the choice of the soul. The soul decides the particular body it would like to inhabit. The varied cultures have evolved over centuries, as did the different races of humanity. If a soul feels most comfortable in a specific way of the body or in a specific culture, it may request to be born into it. All the varied races are requested by the souls and welcomed by the God.

The souls are of different growths. Souls request the bodies of what is most comfortable to them. The body of the varied races is not measurable. The growth of the soul is measurable. The race of humankind is a way of growth. Specific occurrences in the life may have incurred because of the race. These may help the growth and understanding toward God. One race is not more preferable to another in God's eyes. This is the choice of the soul.

Adam and Eve

Did Adam and Eve exist?

Yes, the names were given to souls on Earth who gave birth to sons as recorded. This was not the beginning of the people on Earth but was later in the growth of the world. The story was embellished to give proverb to the masses.

Many stories are true in most ways but are not complete truths. Adam and Eve (sometimes referred to as Evelyn) were the first people to inhabit a particular part of the world. This is now under the ocean. These were souls who were given the light of God. The mentions are not true of the serpent. The tale was given as a lesson and was embraced by the masses.

Adam and Evelyn are not fictitious. However, they were only one couple of many volunteering to begin life on Earth. This was a new, dangerous world, yet it was thick with foliage, and all elements were prevalent to sustain life. Adam and Evelyn were from a place called Ourion, a world adorned with more beauty and love than is imaginable. They asked to come to Earth to begin physical propagation.

What happened at the beginning of Earth?

Several things were on Earth in the beginning. The world was a utopia. It is true that the world was a garden with all needed for survival. The men were numbered nine in the beginning. The women were numbered the same. Others joined in, and their number was soon in the hundreds. People came to Earth at different times. They were from worlds near Earth. God chose the souls. They were honored to be chosen.

Were they placed on Earth as adults?

Yes, the souls were chosen from all who asked to explore and live on the new world. The souls were the highest and most courageous. The world of Earth was supplied with food and also warmth from the Sun, but it was not a world that could be tamed. The communication with God was not obvious, as on other worlds. All was unseen and unheard.

Why is God continually creating souls?

Energy must be utilized. Intelligence must be directed. Movement must continue. Creation is always gaining momentum. Creation is always moving forward. Creation multiplies. Life will always continue, always grow, always — more and more, better and better. Life continues growth forever. The movements shall not cease.

The Sound of Creation

Each soul emits a light. When a soul's light is compatible with a particular world, the soul will feel most comfortable in that world. Earth gives light on a low level. Other worlds have brightness emitting from them. The soul goes through many lives and many levels of growth. When the soul evolves to a higher state where it is no longer in sadness, fear, anger, or hatred and in which love and joyousness are the natural state of mind, the light will shine for all the universe to see.

Each soul gives out a light and a sound that is heard in all the universe. Each word has a tonal quality. The sound is a level of the quality of thought of all people on Earth. It tells all entities in the universe which level of development the whole Earth has accrued. The sounds of all souls are blended to give the sound of Earth. It is now a sound of turmoil and fear. It is not music. It is chaos. The day will come that it will be a beautiful sound.

Your Earth has a welling noise because of the fear and anger on it. The noise is becoming louder, but it's subdued by angels visiting. This will not be quenched in your lifetime, but it can be further subdued. When hate is replaced by acts of good, the noise will cease. Earth needs the help of angels and the inhabitants of other worlds to help calm the pain. We hear the pain of humankind and are with you to help in ways unknown to you. In the past, the sound of Earth was a steady hum of growth, but this is no longer.

The motion of Earth is not in sync with the other worlds. The sound vibration of Earth is not in accordance with other worlds. The motion of the sound emanates with the dimness of the light into an implosion on Earth.

Earth needs much help. People must change themselves from within through thought enhancement and feeling the depth of their souls. They must send forth thoughts of wonder into the atmosphere to help others. This must be done on Earth, for humankind has adversely affected all life on Earth in ways not welcomed by the heavens.

Sound has an impact on the mind. Loud, crass, hammering sounds harm the delicate membranes of the mind. Brash noises can keep the mind focused in a low realm of thought. The mind cannot lift from the lowly spectrum. Certain sounds can lift the consciousness of the mind to encompass the lighter, loftier levels of thought. Should you be exposed to the softness of these sounds daily, it can keep the thought focused in a way to perceive God's wisdom.

Take great care in what sounds are absorbed by the mind. It has extreme influence on the mind. As the soul lifts toward God, music and sounds higher than human understanding will be heard by the soul. You can hear the sweet sounds of all creation. This is beautiful in all ways. Souls of heaven are with us to express the joys in the heavens. We are not to give these sounds to those on Earth. This is a wonder the souls of Earth can experience when they are lifted to God.

Make a Wish

How do we obtain our deepest desires?

You will now learn how to make this happen. You will begin by thinking of a wish. You must clarify the wish, making it as definite as possible. Picture the fulfillment of the desire in all detail. Feel how you will react when this is fulfilled. Do this many times a day. Your desire is on its way to becoming a reality!

Make sure this will not harm anyone. This is important because of the way it is to come about. It must not be against the world's plans. Every action is in accordance with every other action in the world. If it feels correct and will harm no one, you may command the fulfillment of the desire. A way to receive the gifts is to give thanks for all things received. All ways of receiving gifts will be revealed. All ways to receive the wonders of the world are in your grasp.

Another way to receive the gifts of the world is to pray to God. This will be received and delegated to the holy angels. It is given to the angels who determine what is to be given to that person in that lifetime. The desire is not always given. Many things are weighed and will be looked at with consideration.

To realize your desires, picture them most detailed in the mind. Ask the Lord, the Father in heaven, to help you receive these great gifts. Wait and expect these gifts to come to you. When your gifts are received, be thankful. While you await them, good things will come about because this is a creation of the heavens on Earth.

Angels of God will be working to make your will a reality. You need do nothing but wait for the wonders. Sometimes a person waits hundreds of years to realize his or her desires. To know a thought with importance and to know and fulfill all your desires is a great wonder. We will wait with all knowledge. Your dreams will tell us of your deepest desires.

When a soul wants for nothing and understands all things, loves all things, and blesses all things, it is deserving of a place among the gods. This can be attained by any soul. Let it be known that you should aspire to be as a god. Be loving and giving when it is difficult to do so. The God in the heaven shall know of this. One day, you will see God. You will be joyous and exalted in God's presence.

CHAPTER SIX

The Evolution of the Soul

What do you mean when you talk about the "soul"?

A person who feels deeply is opening the heart to pain and to love. The deepest emotions live within the soul's heart. When the soul's heart is incapable of penetration, the soul knows no feeling. This halts soul growth. Let the love in the deep soul pour out to all who can be affected by this intense love. This openness will bring you closer to feeling God.

When we speak of the "movement of the heart," understand that the heart is not only the physical tissue but also the heart of the soul, which has feelings deeper than the mind can fathom. You are soul. When we speak of you, we speak of the enduring soul, not the physical body. The physical body is not you but rather an expression of your soul. In the human body, the physical and the soul grow together in consciousness. It is a place the soul may experience a physical life.

The soul has a heart and a mind. It's subtler than the physical, but it is the true self. The most wonderful words come from the soul's mind because it exists for all time. The soul is to be nurtured as your true self. Listen to the thoughts, and experience the feelings from your soul. The soul thinks, feels, and knows all.

The body is only a shell of the physical to use for the expression of the soul. To realize this, to be aware of this, is a way to be the soul you are and to live as this soul. We are not to interfere, but we will ask you to experience the soul, to bring your soul closer to God. Be the finest, greatest person you can be on this Earth. The God in the heavens will look at you with pride and happiness. Live this life as joyously as possible.

God is always with you. He is ever bringing you toward the

blossoming of your soul. God communicates by way of the holy angels of God. The most important words we want to tell you are these: Open your soul. Surrender your soul to God. Ask God to lead you to truth, love, and peacefulness. Ask God for any attributes you wish to acquire. God's angels will help you become the strong, powerful soul that you are meant to become.

A world of souls lifting their minds to reach God will affect the universe. Be the soul you are meant to be. The most powerful attribute a soul may attain is love. Love is felt in the strongest intensity and is given to God or other beings. Emulate the qualities of the gods in the heavens. People of Earth can't see the gods, so they must pray to God to know the equalities of the heart, which the gods may nurture.

Are souls born in heaven?

Yes, souls are manifested first in the heavens. God creates the new souls. The souls created are then brought to existence for all eternity.

The Physical Body on Earth

Which is more important: life in a body or the soul alone?

The life on Earth and the lives in the heavens or other strata are all of importance. One is no more important than another. All are paths to God.

When a life ends on Earth, the soul might be needed in another place, as the life is eternal. Rebirth on Earth or another world is given by request if it is in accordance with the growth of the soul. Any other path requested can still be attained. Anything may be discussed with the angels, and then the soul can be prepared to enter a body.

Is it possible to live forever in a body?

All will live forever not in a body but in heaven. When those on Earth want to make it as a heaven, the souls may live in bodies on Earth forever. It's possible to live in the body forever on other worlds. In a moment in time, in worlds unknown by people of Earth, the way will be given to a brother of humankind to give to others. The way to live in the body through eternity will be given. This will not be given to the people of Earth for many eons. Why would one want to live in one body forever instead of growing into new bodies? New lives keep the movement of change and growth alive.

Ask God for a New Beginning

How can we lift the soul?

Only the sincerity of thought is required to lighten and soften the soul into refinement. You need only the desire to lift closer to God. Most of you humbly ask God to help you through your thoughts or words. God may send angels to you to give blessings, but you may not see or hear them.

You do not need a person of the cloth to give these blessings. The cleansing is to confess the unwanted things of the soul. Ask God to remove the burdens and give the soul a new beginning. God, most merciful, will give this to the wanting soul. Let this be not words of no feeling, for it will not be given credence.

The most important plan in your mind should be to lift the soul to God by asking him to help you to be better and to create the world as he deems. Each soul on Earth is doing things to affect the world, whether it is positive or negative. Rather than destroy, each of you should create the world you envision. Ask God for what you need.

Is there such a thing as "translated beings"?

The term "translated beings" was coined by a religion to help bring an aura of secrecy to the teachings, thereby enticing the followers to yearn for more knowledge. Death may come unexpectedly or be planned by the soul over decades. God holds no soul dearer than another at the end of life on Earth.

One may suffer greatly or not at all at the end of life. At times, angels may enter the soul before an accident occurs to lift the soul. We always hold the soul at the death of the body. This is for all souls. The more enlightened the soul, the more quickly it lifts with the angels. To tarry or hover around the body is not desirable.

At the end of life, pain may be necessary and warranted. In many deaths, ways of God are sought to subdue or omit pain. This is through prayer. One is not chosen over another to alleviate pain. This is all from the soul's own thoughts and expectations.

The term "translated" is human-made. This brings followers of the church the hope that they might, at the end of life on Earth, become angels and do works of God upon the Earth.

Do any souls become angels after death?

No souls are preferred to become as ministering angels. God appoints angels over viewing hundreds of lifetimes. Earth is a low form of existence. This is not to say this can't be done, but it would be most rare.

Those of a church are not to hold themselves as having more sanctity than any other souls. The angels' words shall bring truths to the world and free the followers of God from reverence to those who profess secret knowledge of God's ways. All that is needed is within your own soul; bring to God all that you are, and God will welcome you. Lift with the holy angels when the last breath is inhaled.

At the moment of death, the soul will choose its destiny: to stay in the body, to lift with the angels, or to wander Earth as a spirit with no light of God. Spirits have no powers to help on Earth. Angels of God hold the light of God and move about Earth. Hold the soul in the highest homage to God. Lift to him and serve him. Do not be afraid.

To remain on Earth is a regrettable path of ignorance and fear. We hold these truths before God and humankind. This must be known that the soul must always move toward God in all ways.

Do animals have souls?

Yes, they have souls — not in the evolved way as humans, but the soul survives the death on Earth that is the lowest of all birthplaces. New life is constantly created in all forms. God creates the eternal souls who seek any body to house the soul. This is given as requested.

Heaven is always housing new creations. Souls can hear, think, see, speak, and feel without a body. They only request a physical body when they move into a new life on other worlds. Some souls give no discretion as to what body they inhabit. They will be able to respond physically in any body. The growth is self-determined.

Can you explain consciousness of the soul?

This is explainable as the growth of the soul. The soul is as a cloud of vapor in your shape with your physical attributes. The soul thinks, speaks, feels, hears, acts, behaves, moves, see, flies, walks, dances, laughs, and sings. The soul is identical to a physical body except that it lives after the human body dies.

Every emotion you feel is felt by the soul. The soul can become as a solid human or can remain as a wisp of translucence. Consciousness is the growth of the heart of the soul and the mind of the soul. These integrate to develop an essence of refinement of the consciousness. A person of no feeling and of crudeness or grossness will have a low level of consciousness. A person of self-worth, discipline, and dignity will have a higher level of consciousness. This is a measurement of the growth of the synchrony of the soul's mind and heart.

Does consciousness have light?

Yes, the lower the level, the lower the emission of luminosity. The higher the soul evolution, the brighter and more luminous the soul. This is seen by all in the heavens. A life in the heavens is met by souls of all levels of development, as is life on Earth. The soul is exactly as created by the mind of the soul.

People of great worth walk with gods and with angels. Angels are everywhere in the heavens and can be seen in many pursuits, many endeavors. All are serving God in varied ways. Angels have diverse interests.

Soul Qualities

As the soul evolves, the aspects of what is considered supernatural to those of Earth become natural movements of the evolved soul and will steer toward true desires. When a soul reaches heaven, all past lives are revealed. Desires may change when all knowledge is absorbed and understood. In heaven, you can make decisions from a fuller and higher perspective. The souls of Earth have much to learn. Qualities of the mind and heart must be developed in all ways.

Truth: All is truth in the heavens. All is made true in all ways. We honor those who are truthful in moments of adversity; those who know that truth will cause them pain of death but who choose to be honest in all ways. This is a most coveted quality of the soul. Of all things, truth is the most respected attribute among all people. Stand behind your word, for you will be exalted in the heavens.

Truth is a possession of the soul. When it becomes a part of you, it's a tremendous step forward. It's a movement of the soul more coveted than any other. It's held high over your head like a beaming glow, envied by lesser people. Truth in the face of punishment is viewed with amazement and noted well among the angels. Truth stands tall and straight. It cannot be moved, deterred, conjured, or deceived, for it's fulfilled within itself.

Only on the level of God and the absolute heavenly strata exists truth in absolute purity. On Earth, truths exist and are known and experienced. Everything in life is a reflection of the level of the individual soul. It is the same with truth. Truth is only as it can be perceived on Earth and only by the soul's level of awareness. The soul will know truths as if unfolding perceptions.

Honesty: When the soul gives up theft and accumulation of material possessions, it makes way for the paths of gifts from the heavens. As the desire to covet declines, the soul acquires possessions in the way of powers one would otherwise not possess. This is to be given as you restrain yourself from theft, from desiring another's possessions. The honest soul is a soul more treasured by the angels than can be imagined, for this soul's word is his bond.

An honest soul is trusted beyond any boundary. It does not steal, nor lie. It is honored among angels. An honest soul has a light that emanates brightly. Its glory is for all to know and to see in all worlds and in the heavens. A soul who can be trusted with another's life is a soul of greatness.

Integrity: A person of integrity is someone who cannot be bribed, bought, cajoled, or corrupted. This soul is of honor and truth. This is a most admirable value of the self. This brings the soul into completeness and wholeness to lift toward God. The wellness of the soul is a treasured thing. The plan of humankind is for all souls to integrate integrity into life on Earth.

Trust: One of the highest qualities is the trust of your word. If you say a word, let it be that all souls know it's the truth. Let all souls know, with their lives, your word is all that need be known. People who stand behind their thoughts and words stand tall and firm in the eyes of all who view them. To gain a person's trust and to know that person's word can be counted on is the strongest, most honorable bond you can own.

Trust is an armament stronger than any metal, more treasured than any gem. It's a comfort of the soul that frees the mind to expression, for without it, there is pain and fear, doubt and troubles.

Let trust be as much a part of your conduct and your countenance as your knowing the Sun rises in the morning. No one can strip you of the qualities of your soul. Trust is part of an honorable person.

Respect: It's a loving thing to give courteous respect to people of worth. To give this respect to all humans is a difficult order. Each soul in a human body deserves respect for having the courage to be born on Earth. Each human is on Earth to perform a specific task of the soul, even if this is only known between him and the angels. All minds are to be tolerated for growth in the human body. To give respect to those who feel they deserve none is to give them honor.

The way to give respect is to approach with humbleness, or give reverence in a manner allowing honor and dignity to the soul. To give honor to all God's children is to honor God and God's angels.

Love: Love on Earth is necessary to open the feelings encased in the heart. If you have lost in love, this opens the heart to understanding and then to openness of compassion, depth of love, and movement of the soul.

Courage: Courage is the act of giving one's body to deliver something needed by the soul. It's a release of fear, of inevitability to the making of an action. Whether it is fighting a battle or an act of heroism or whether it is testing one's mettle or risking one's life, it's a growth of the soul. It's something needed by the soul in this life. A courageous soul is a soul most welcome in the heavens.

The way to attain courage of the soul is to ask God for bravery. Realize anything that can hurt you can only hurt the physical body, not your soul. The soul can rise above the occurrences that happen on Earth.

Live in your soul, not in your body. Don't be afraid of the future.

Wonders can only occur to the soul if the soul has no fear. A way to make sure no fear can take hold is to always move toward God by knowing you are strong. You can endure all things for what is right. If you did not know this in the past, you are not held accountable. Now you know the right action to take to hold steadfast to your soul's truths and not be afraid of harm for being as you are. Be strong; be without fear of any person.

Faith: People of the world will always give hope to the unseen and unheard. Faith is a remembrance of what was experienced before this life and a promise to yourself of what will come. The soul desires. The soul hopes. The soul dreams of all that heaven avows.

Faith is a realization of the mind — to believe in something the senses cannot feel, that the intellect cannot deduce. This is only a promise. The soul knows. Faith is the inner knowledge of truth.

The Most Important Quality

The most valuable asset one can acquire is to become a person of quality and reverence toward God. Being a person of quality brings in attributes you must acquire during life. It's not to float through life having fun. You must give yourself to others. Make the world better for anyone other than yourself.

Acquiring prosperity is not to be the main goal in life. Acquiring attributes to elevate the soul to a higher level is much more important. Know that all will be given in the heavens. Immediate gratification on Earth is not needed.

The life on Earth is not to be used in a fruitless manner. Be aware that God is here. Be aware that angels are here. Behave as if you were in the presence of the highest entity in all places. Objects of desire are without meaning. Instead, build your thoughts to be able to alter energy. This is a power that you will have after this life. Make your thoughts strong enough so that anyone without perception can hear your thoughts. Send love and healing to all people of the world who are in need.

It's not wrong to possess many things, but you should focus more on building your strength within and feeling love and compassion for others. Sending this love to them is much more important that material possessions. Thoughts can be originated into constructive, powerful, directed ways to change or influence your surroundings. Prayer to God is an example of sending thought. Feelings and emotions with strong, directed thought are in sincere prayers.

The Power of Thought

It's most important that people of Earth learn to strengthen the force of thought. This is done by letting the mind think a specific thought. Don't say the thought aloud but bring the thought to maximum loudness without speaking it. As this technique is practiced, it will become almost audible to someone nearby. This will clarify the thought so that the thoughts are no longer muddled in the mind.

This method must be used in the future. It's imperative that this this be prepared for future occurrences. This is deliberate thought. The thought gains power, as it is not lessened by speech. This clear, focused thought will be used to help others. When the time arrives, those who are of awareness and spiritual development will use this, so this power won't be used for other than the ways of good.

This is the beginning of the powers people will utilize in the future. Many wonders and many fulfillments will come from this exercise of the mind. The next phase of this is to send the thought. When it reaches the maximum force, you are to send this to another person by focusing on the mind receiving the thought.

Make the first thought of the day directed to God. This will set the mood for the day because blessings and thanksgivings will be sent and received. When the mind is in a state of receiving blessings, wonders may occur.

Most will not address God unless an occurrence compels them to ask for help. We speak now of the thought levels. Prayer raises the level of thought in the mind; therefore, to give thought and prayer to God in the rising time of the body will set a movement of energy conducive to harmony in the surroundings.

This is not a prayer of fear. This is a feeling of thankfulness that will ultimately help the world. If souls of Earth knew the power they have with the movement of thought, studies would be taught of the formation of strong thought. One powerful thought generated from one mind can change the entire world. It can cause miracles to occur. It can induce wonders in the life and the lives of others.

Lifting Others' Thoughts

Can we make others lift their thoughts?

No soul can make another rise in thought unless the mind is willing. You could prepare a speech of the greatest thought, and it would fall on deaf ears. You could plead that others would hear the words of the heavens, but no one would be there to understand. This is fine, for the thought of God will penetrate the world's atmosphere.

Listen to our words: You, as a soul of Earth, are to lift other souls to see God and to feel God's presence. This is how to show others through your words and actions that you are not only a servant of God but also a leader of humanity. Be the person you would like all people to replicate. This will spread, and multitudes will be of greatness. Oh, what glorious wonders will occur on Earth as each person begins to know God within his or her own being.

Do you believe in God? Do you fear God? This is how to experience God! Now, as God watches, you should not only be a follower of God but also a disciple! Yes, this can be done! This is not done by following others. This is done by bearing your entire soul to God. You are to give God the best of you and the worst of you. You are not to evaluate the things happening around you with a closed heart. If you close off the light of God or close up any thought of love, all you will know is bitterness and misery.

Change

Can you tell us about change?

Change is a movement that is mentioned by time, space, and the actions of all minds. Any way the movement is brought is a change that is neither good nor bad. It's only different from previous experiences. You should be open to the acceptance of change, as it brings new concepts to your life.

Let change stem from a forward movement. Let new ideas and new concepts form. Let the new be welcomed. There is no stopping movement. All is in constant change. Embrace it. Smile on it. Make something wonderful from it. Change will always be a constant. Move with it, and give it positive support.

Can we affect the world?

Tell the people the most important plan in the human mind should be to lift the soul to God by asking God to help them be better and to create the world as he deems. Each soul on Earth is doing things to affect the world, whether it is positive or negative. Rather than destroy, you each should create the world you envision.

Ask God for what you need. A most important value you can attain is wisdom. Wisdom is a combination of intellect, knowledge, and common sense. You should use the brain to decipher thoughts of credibility, and use words carefully to ensure credibility and honesty. Be knowledgeable of the areas of discernment. Consider all factors being affected by the words uttered. Give thought to all aspects. Speak strongly without faltering in your beliefs and ideas.

Bring the Eternal Soul Forward

People of Earth want dearly to have powers beyond Earthly capabilities. Such powers will not rise above the consciousness of the world as a whole. At a time in the future when you receive the others with love and joy, the world's love will lift your thoughts to use powers beyond what is now achievable. People who have achieved these ways were sent here as teachers. However, they would be more comfortable in another world.

Human minds are limited in the ways of intelligence. There are no people who can say they have used their full potential, even in the genius qualities. So much more lies in the human mind that will be utilized in the future. Moments of lucidness can reveal what human potential is capable of. Some experience this in fleeting thought. Many years in the future, the human mind will be developed so that thought will be known throughout civilizations. No speech will be necessary but will still be used. What is now considered superpowers will be natural movements for all humankind. Much knowledge of science must be obtained before this will occur.

Many will dream of the challenges of the future. Know these dreams will someday be realities. More wonderful inventions than can be imagined will become realities. Create visions of ideals with the mind. Envision ways you desire the world to progress.

Pleasures of the Soul

Dismiss the pattern of self-indulgence of the mind and body from the soul. As this is done, the realization of spiritual powers will begin in the expression of the soul. The more you integrate the awareness of God and the goal to reach God, the more wonders will enter your life. These are pleasures of the soul rather than the lusts of self-indulgence.

Spiritual powers will come in a natural manner, not by force. The movements will come as the soul grows closer to becoming the soul it desires in the heart. This is the bringing of the eternal soul to the fore in everyday life. The will of the force of thought will disregard evilness, bring compassion to the saddened, and uplift the righteous.

The wavering moods of the mind are ever fluctuating and can be steadied by seeking not only God but also to be a clean, joyful soul for God to view. Cheerfulness honestly felt can be a reflection of the qualities of the heart, but the presence of ecstasy can be falsified to bring others to that particular faith. If this persists in your aloneness, religion may be truly fulfilling you, for the true joy comes from lifting the heart and mind to God.

People of Earth holding to the highest self-examination of truth and cleanliness are preparing their souls to receive the one God and God's attributes. Make the will of God your will, and new ways to God will be revealed. This awakening rejuvenates your soul.

By sacrificing the eternal soul for fleeting pleasures of the exterior, the mortal is missing a chance to lift the soul and grow in God. To attain all spiritual powers, you need to become calm, peaceful, and serene in the ways of God. The individual remains but grows to the luminous, pure self. This is a radiant creation of soul growth.

The attainment of the qualities of the soul through selflessness, courage, love, and holiness radiate from the heart to other hearts. These qualities are self-taught on Earth to adorn the eternal soul in the heavens. No mention of the sins of humanity is to be dwelled on. Rather, integrate the opposite. Bring forth the qualities desired in the soul. To rid the ignorances in the darkness, integrate the light. Let each soul be aware of the pureness of heart it is capable of attaining. Once you shed fears and feelings of worthlessness, you can see yourself becoming a person of courage, honor, and quality.

Realization of each soul must include knowledge that you need not attain all desires on Earth. Life is eternal. Build the soul into personal enlightenment, and all will be yours. You will not think of the repercussions of an act or word but be aware that this life is not the only life. This is only a page of an eternal existence in the radiant heavens.

Ask for Spiritual Power

Qualities of the heart will be gained as people develop into a higher species. This is necessary for entrance to the higher worlds. Before you can materialize objects with what is now considered supernatural powers, the qualities of the soul's heart and mind need to grow and be utilized. Angels give these qualities freely. All you need to do is ask God, humbly and sincerely.

Angels delight in bringing the development of these qualities to the soul. Prayer is the beginning of higher powers because telepathy begins with strength of thought. Prayer to God is a preparation to develop this strength and clarity of thought. This practice defines the thought. This will be necessary to communicate in higher worlds.

Can you pray for these attributes?

Calmness, kindness, empathy, compassion, intelligence, wisdom, generosity, love, tenderness, gentleness, strength, courage, happiness, thankfulness, grace — the aspects of the soul are many, and you cannot override the beginnings of the attributes in order to know the powers desired. The heart knows more love than can be expressed on Earth. Love is in the deepest recesses of the soul's heart and is unending. This will be experienced when you give yourself to God.

The creations and manifestations of the physical are possible but only by angelic or heavenly creations. People on Earth cannot create in this way because of the low thought level in the world. The other functions of the mind are possible but only if you have gained the aspects of the soul.

Miracles on Earth

How do miracles occur?

A miracle will happen in a life when the angels declare it is the best way to help a person. Sometimes we give help in ways not recognized as natural. These should not be mentioned to others unless told to do so. They should be cherished as works of angels under God.

Miracles are true happenings using God's powers to bring a significant change that wouldn't ordinarily happen. Angels try other ways to communicate with you. When these communications fail and it's determined change must occur, we will cause the change.

All miracles transcend human reason. Any wonderful thing can happen at any time. Be ready for it and expect it because any moment of life is special. Angels have the power of miracles. Some angels tend love and healing in ways that soothe the sorrows and pains. The release of anger heals the body in specific ways. By letting go of the hidden thoughts holding you back, energy shifts to a positive movement, enacting wonders in the life. Let go of boundaries of belief systems and social conditioning. You are a most unique soul.

Do God's Work on Earth

Do we emit light like the angels do?

The light of angels is an emanation of God. This is a field of energy we use in many ways. Your world is a lowly world. It gives light on a low level.

Each soul emits a light. When the soul's light is compatible with that world, the soul will feel most comfortable there. Other worlds have brighter lights emitting from them. When a soul is bright, this soul will feel comfortable in that particular world.

The soul goes through many lives and many levels of growth. When the soul evolves to a higher state where it is no longer in a state of sadness, fear, anger, or hatred and in which love and joy are the natural state of the mind, the light will shine for all the universe to see.

In a world of weakened souls, you are to lift out of the despondency to make the world better for anyone. Lift your heart to God. When the heart lifts the light of the soul, it's visible for all entities to view. Angels will surround the soul.

The light of the soul is alive with vibrancy. The glow is seen by angels and entities alike. All powers rush in to view the luminosity. All possibilities open to you, for there is a boldness and strength in lifting to meet God in thought. The action of the mind to enact wonders can bring miracles to the soul.

The minds are now entangled in lowly thought. The human mind has infinite possibilities, beginning with producing a thought. People tend to desire more happiness and more prosperity for themselves. This is fine, but the mind and thoughts are designed to be used more importantly. The human mind is in its infancy.

It must be known that to give to another over yourself is not only a tremendous boost for the soul, but the gods, the angels, and all entities about you will flood to your soul as well. The soul now emits a new, different light. When a thought comes into the mind that benefits another soul over itself, entities of the heavens are attracted and rush to view the circumstances. Not only does each soul emit light but also a sound that is heard by those in the heavens.

An organized, preplanned movement is given to the soul before birth. When there is a deviation of significant growth, we angels surround the soul as our charge on Earth is lifted to a higher purpose. This is a most wonderful movement of energy. We angels are lifted into more and more bliss.

All who read and understand this shall be lifted to meet God in the soul, for multitudes of angels surround Earth at this time. Angels stand before you and surround you. Let your words and actions be worthy of our viewing. Plan all movements in accordance with the loving thoughts of angels.

Should people fall into pitiful uselessness, let them choose now to rise above this and hold themselves high as Children of God in all ways. Should sloth and decrement decorate your being, cleanse them from it into the light of God. Should fanciful mirth of no purpose overtake you, shake it off in solemn prayer. What lies before you is a road not to be paved in ignorance but in planned, purposeful thought. Hold the momentary pleasures, for all will be given in time. Lift instead to stand with the angels in wholeness.

An army of the highest magnificence is unfolding on Earth. These angels will be surrounding all souls in both seen and unseen manners. Live as though they are beside you. Thoughts are heard. Works are noted. Lives are given to God. All is God's. If all of your past lived no more from this second forward, you could stand with angels as an emissary of God. Now and for all time, you will decide your movements. You will choose to live in purpose and in value in the life of the soul given to God. Stand with all beings.

The Words of Archangel Michael

God in the heavens wants to make a world of much growth. He wants to make a world of much love and peace, but the world has not responded. Good people of Earth, please listen to the following words: Be yourself in your spirit, for you are a most honored soul and know the truths and the falsehoods. You know the ways of the gods are now given.

You are waiting for a realization but all that is needed is within and also given by the angels surrounding you. Life on this Earth is so important in the sacred ways of God. Let the world know the ways of God are now without the wants of avarice. The world is not to want for God's words.

When the feelings of God are experienced in even the subtlest ways, human minds open the heart of the soul. The life is with God in the strata of wisdom and love. When you open your soul to be lifted to God, let go of despair, anger, avarice, and fear. The most crucial action at this time is to pray to God for peacefulness and harmony in the world. This is imperative at this time on Earth.

A way to lift to God is to not hold the self above all others. The sincerity and humbleness of the human heart will beg in promise and cry in hopefulness before the one God in the heavens. This will be heard and understood by God.

The words of God will be dispersed to souls of a questioning nature. This is an honor not to be dismissed. God has directed these words that are now to be given to the people of Earth. May all receive and give worth to the heavenly words. The actions and workings of people are necessary and are not without merit.

All interactions are purposeful. All people's creations have purpose, as creation prepares the soul to create in the heavens. People are to live with each other in unity. Feel with the other. Let your kindness flow to others. The world is to be a mention of God's mercy. Be merciful to the people as God is merciful to you.

CHAPTER SEVEN

The New Spirituality

This moment begins the you who possesses no fear, no hate, no pain of repercussions, no slovenly habits, no telling of untruths, and no holding on to painful memories. This is a release of all that is not you in your highest being. The life you will create from this moment forward is now the path toward the one God. This path is with all wonders. This is the way of truth in all things, causing no harm — even in the tiniest way — through words, actions, or thoughts. This will open the way to the new beginning for you and all who do this.

This is the beginning of the person you *must* become. A lifetime of bitterness, complaints, and anger can all be diminished by thought. The life you are to live now is to be the most wonderful life you can conceive. Let it be no less. Why wait another moment to make your life begin its wonderfulness? Your world begins at this moment. Even a moment in the past should not be given any merit.

Use this life as a way to grow in character, not just to receive things from the world. Be in harmony with all who are around you, and know this is the normal way. Let the ways of the angels give you words, power, and strength. The new movement of the spirit of humankind has begun. People will now begin to express thoughts and words that are a step higher in communications. People will now lift the quality of thought to send messages of love to all souls of the world.

Open expression of feelings will now come about in many people. Secrets will be revealed to the world. The most prevalent method to do this is to discuss God openly. The values each person holds will be unveiled. Truths will be understood. The most essential component of this is truth. Even if truth is given to the assured reaction of punishment, it must be given before all things. All people will stand before God and tell the secrets of their hearts and souls.

Understanding and forgiveness will be given to the masses bearing the transgressions of the soul. A new world will come of this action. A world of no lies and no deception — only truthfulness and honesty — will lighten the souls of all to lift higher to God. The soul will unburden itself of secrets. The most wonderful events will begin to happen on Earth.

The soul is made free by letting go of pain and hate. This gives way for wonders to enter the life. The contentment in unveiling your transgressions is a step toward the realization of God's miracles. A soul must confess only to God and tell of what it no longer wants as part of its soul. Ask God to remove the pain, the hate, the fears, and all that should not be in the most perfect soul.

Will Your Desires into Life

How do we receive wonders in our lives?

A new way of believing is coming. We are to bring the secrets of the gods to you now. Make a world in which you would want to live. Think of what you want to happen in your life, why you want it to happen, and then create it in your life. Think beyond your own needs. Think of your country and of the world. You can change the way you relate to people. Think what you want in the course of your life. The moments cannot be kept to mend the past. Now is the time to experience.

The future isn't here, but it can be planned to a degree. The hope of better days is a strong mind enhancer. If it turns out not to be what is hoped, the will to live on is here to sustain. Souls tend to have hope for tomorrow. You can always have the will to continue. Live fully in the moment now.

We are here to tell you the most wonderful way to receive the wonders of life: When a desire comes into the mind, you are to make it a command. Will it to come into life. By doing this, you not only bring it to the mind through thought but also reinforce it by making it a command.

When a prayer is answered, the plan is to wait until the time is right to receive gifts from God. Many gifts are given after this life. When we help you plan this life, we fulfill the ways of God and are his servants. A soul will only receive what has been preplanned before the birth of the soul. We try to fulfill prayers but are under strict order.

How can we experience this part of God within us?

Make each day more wonderful than the last. Give thanks for each new day. Make your time count so that you are thankful for each moment spent on Earth. One day, you will see yourself as others see you.

Try to look at your actions as if you were the other person. Be the way you want others to see and hear you. Be aware of your words and actions, and know that you are the way you pretend. Find wonders in your life. Find things for which you are thankful. You create your days and nights. The way you respond to happenings, the way you interact with others, and the way you use your moments are all important.

When all things around you are in chaos or in sadness, find ways to comfort or words to calm. Find actions to help, even in little ways. Try to make all moments better. Try to help in any way possible. It may be difficult to give thanks for some moments, but look at things from different viewpoints instead of being caught in dissatisfied emotion.

Reach inside to realize the importance of others, and know that they are meant to be with you at a particular time in your life. When you realize how you would feel if they weren't there, you can sometimes love them more. Reach into your heart to love all who surround you. Give of yourself in your thoughts. Let yourself feel compassion and gentleness for all souls.

Live gently. Be tickled by the whisperings rising softly in your soul. Let joy unveil the sheltered beauty deep within your gentle soul. Don't be afraid to feel deeply. Let yourself feel. Let your eyes tear. Be vulnerable to the world. Shield not your emotions. When you love, you will find there is no end but the peaceful remnants of loving and forgiving.

Expressing thankfulness to the one God, the Son of God, and all the angels surrounding you is the way to feel the depth of love within. All the gods in the heavens will feel your thankfulness. All gods will bend to know the love in your soul. Think of ways to make anything better, even in the most insignificant ways. Think of each day as an opportunity to help others. Try to make each day a new wonder for you and all around you. Lift your heart to God each new day. Let your actions and words be a sacred homage to the glory of God.

Call your angels to help you through difficult situations. Angels help in all ways. Angels stand with you to help and comfort you. Know they are always with you. You will not be alone in any endeavor. While you are in times of repose, they will try to communicate with you. Give thanks for their presence. Give of yourself in your thoughts. Let yourself feel compassion and gentleness for all souls.

The Importance of Thought

How and why do we lift our thoughts?

It's important to carry only thoughts of wonderment. Using thought to condemn and hate only brings despair to the mind. The choice is clear. If thoughts of goodness fill the mind, this will bring goodness into the life. Forgive, and the heaviness of the dark thoughts leaves the body, and the body lightens.

The soul lifts higher toward the heavens. A great weight is lifted from the soul, and when it lifts to the heavens, it can go on to new things rather than be bound by the ways of the past. So many delights await the heaven bound. The mind of the soul wants to be set free. The ways of God are given, but the human mind can reject the glories and remain in despair. The soul can choose quality of life on Earth.

When the world lifts each thought to reflect the will of God, the world will blossom in intelligence, in wisdom, and in love. Joy will prevail over all things. Wars will be no more. Kindness will be in all hearts. Ways of all wonders will be experienced the world over. People will sicken at the thought of war. People will begin to pray to God as not before in Earth's history, for they will know the wonders are God's gifts to humankind.

Discoveries will unfold in the atmosphere of Earth. They are not at a high quotient of energy now, so minds must struggle to receive them. As Earth provides the higher thought patterns, the discoveries will be received by human minds.

Love, creations, and wonders will reappear on Earth. This all begins with each soul stopping thoughts that are of no benefit to humankind. As thoughts come into the mind, they go through a discriminating area of discernment.

When the thinker becomes aware of the thought, he or she can choose to speak it aloud, save it to memory, or discard it as useless. When the thought is lowly, it's better for the entire world to not speak it aloud. Let it go from the mind as not worthy to speak. If discernment were given to thought as it is to speech, human minds would be on a higher level. Ignorance would be replaced by wisdom and peacefulness.

Words

Speak the words you would want your surrounding angels to hear. We know your thoughts. We exalt at your holding thoughts of harm or of no purpose rather than speaking them. Envision a world where kindness overrides hate, where wisdom is lifted over ignorance, and where criticism is replaced by good wishes. A world as this will be closer to God and God's wonders. Souls of Earth look to leaders of countries to bring peace, but this cannot happen.

Words are powerful. Be most careful with all words. The moment a word creates a bad emotion, it may stay in the mind, causing disease. All words will now be lifted to a level of great worth. This is the word spoken from humanity as the word given from angels. We angels give the word of God to the people of Earth, and when heeded, we are in such joy.

When you speak with clear mental processes, the voice is unwavering, undiminished, and wise. This is to be endeavored by the people of Earth. One must hold words until thought becomes powerful. Words of angels are to be taken as the word of God. This is not to be confused with the mentions of the lowly spirits.

When a thought is made for the good of others over the self, all in the heavens are watching. This is a great strength from people of great honor and actions. You on Earth can decide to be of great worth and of the most principled thought. A person can be more giving than is needed, lift the spirits of all souls addressed, speak ill of no one, and give great power and worth to all utterances.

You Are Responsible for Lifting the Quality of Thought

The human race must move forward in an extraordinary leap of mental and emotional development to bring the entire world out of the continuum of chaotic devolution. If a movement of humans on Earth could develop the mind (the force of thought) and the communication with God and God's angels through the opening of the heart and the depth of feeling, it would help put the world on the path to God again. Create your world: The future of the world is up to the souls inhabiting it. God gave you this world as a gift to live your life as you deem. Why not lift to God and live in the most love and happiness you can create?

Can a soul humble before God and ask to help Earth in any way?

Ask for wisdom, compassion, understanding, and kindness, and as these ways come into the mind, let the human heart grow and express this to the world. Make this day a communication with the heavens. Each person should strive to be this power on Earth not through aggressiveness and manipulation but through the strength of thought and emotional feelings, holding tight to his or her merits of truth and honor and living a life of respect. To be aware of angels around you and to give of yourself to strangers is to be a true person of God.

If you each achieved these changes within yourselves, it would radiate to all the world. This would bring the wonders Earth needs. This is not something you can dismiss. This is a necessity. Human thought must be used to project love to humankind. Souls must feel empathy for fellow humans and for all living creatures in their care. The world needs the love from the souls of Earth. This is more important than you can know! Stand before God to declare that you will help anyone in the world.

Know that you are a Child of God and are worthy in all ways of God's love. See in your mind the most wonderful soul, and be that soul. You have the power to enact wonders in the world. Let this be done! When thoughts are sent, it's the responsibility of each soul to lift the quality of thought. Be most careful of thoughts sent out into the world. You can direct your thoughts. Choose not to cause pain but to effect joy.

A thought sent into the world is now immersed in an ocean of thoughts, which influence the future actions of the entire world. A thought of truth is more important than can be imagined. The future of the world changes with every action. Some things are ordained. When you see the future, you may see these things. Other things may differ in duration or circumstance.

You Can Change the Future through Thought

Many things are changed by thought and physical action. A tremendous occurrence may not even come about because of prayers to God. If the thoughts are so distraught as to affect the outcome of an occurrence, it indeed may worsen. As soon as thoughts are transmitted from the brain, they may be augmented into positive suppositions. It's not natural to think only thoughts of goodness. Cause no harm by your thoughts if at all possible.

Some events cannot be changed but can become less or more by the thoughts moving in the atmosphere. Know that thought may change time as it's known on Earth and can affect events preordained to happen. Thought with feeling and emotion may be needed in this world to hamper destined unfortunate events. When feeling enters the thought, it becomes more powerful.

When the focused thought is propelled through the atmosphere, it can initiate things to happen. This is why many predictions of the future are changed or distorted. Thought interferes with future events. If the people knew the power of the mind to focus and send thought to effect change and wonderment, there would be groups studying this to make the world more wonderful at this time.

A way to do this on an individual basis is to direct thoughts to a specific person. Picture a person as you wish the person to be, and send blessings and love to that person. You may do this for yourself as well. A way to attain the one goal you desire is to picture this already attained.

Humanity is now going through a most difficult period. This is due to the low quality of thought pervading the atmosphere. The mention of thought is dull in the mind, but humanity must address this. They must know the profound effects thought has on what occurs in the world. You must have freedom of thought, motion, and words. Thoughts should now be of the highest, loftiest qualities. Strengthening the force of thought is of much importance. The influx of kindness from the heart of the soul is a consideration in the formation of thought as well.

The Power to Change Your Thoughts

When you find yourself in a low, depressed, saddened level, you must immediately change this program of thought values. Much can be corrected through the diet. It's important not to remain in this lowly state of thought formation. Begin by finding anything in life for which you are thankful. Know that God and your surrounding angels can help you. Pray to God, and ask to be lifted from this state of mind. Angels surround you at this moment. They know your sincerity and help lift you to a calmer, happier state.

The low level of thought needs to be changed and not extended. This permeates the atmosphere and enters minds to keep the level of thought stagnant. Lift the thought. Do not stay in a state of despondency.

Strengthen the thought: To strengthen thought, think the thought as strongly as possible without saying it aloud. This is similar to pulling back the string of a bow before shooting an arrow. Minds receive this strong thought. This gives power to the demeanor. Words do not need to be spoken. Strong thought gives the same influence as words if properly directed.

Direct the thought: To direct thought, picture the person to whom the thought is for. Think of that particular individual, and propel the strong thought toward him or her. Even if not received as words, the perception will be received by the mind. This exercise is needed in future lives, where thought is used as communication.

Work miracles with thought: Kindness and softness from the heart of the soul is brought forth to filter into the quality of thought. Harshness and rashness adds no love to your thoughts. Thought is to be kind and loving but strong and directed. May the words of this inform any who wish to make miraculous results in life.

By utilizing these methods, you can gain abundance, love, and personal desires and achieve wonders in life. Focus must be employed. Kindness must be integrated. Strength of thought must be utilized. The high level of thought quality must be maintained. One must ask God for keeping this endeavor. This keeps the light of God around the goal. Ask God's angels to help guide the soul to keep God in the thought process. When this technique is perfected, the soul has strength of thought that will be needed in the heavens and on other worlds. Were there a way we angels could explain the importance of this movement of thought in the human mind, we would plan events around this.

Change your life: Wake one day and tell yourself that you will not gossip this day. You will not complain. You will not wallow in self-loathing or in despondency. This day, you will rise above the lowly thoughts.

The coming days will begin to offer new changes in life. Momentous occurrences will be possible. The world will be viewed in a different perspective. Wonders will begin to occur. Give thanks for all received — a smile, a kind word, or a gift of thoughtfulness. Give thanks for the works in progress on the way to you for which you have not yet received. They will come to you.

A Secret to Diffuse Hate

In order to disuse thoughts of hate, send disarming thoughts and visions to those who inspire this feeling. Instead of spiteful thoughts, send joyful feelings to them with thought progression. It will be received and understood that a thought of love can do more than you can know to help heal the soul of one in need. Give these thoughts freely. Create them. Strengthen them until they are powerful, and send them to the saddened hearts. In your experience, when a bad occurrence appears to you, you must remember that you have the power to turn the situation around. Use this event to utilize the power of the mind to create positive effects.

When you feel someone sending hate to you, send your most powerful thoughts of love to diffuse the situation. Immediately pull the love from within and picture the person as joyful, loving, and receptive — feeling wonderful. Spend not one moment in a response that is defensive. Know the person is receiving the love you send. It's a miraculous secret all humanity should practice. The repercussions will be felt all over the world. Practice this whenever a moment of discordance appears in your life. Do not react to events; cause events.

Lift your heart to know God. Use this love to send joyous thoughts to those you have disagreements with, knowing they will be received. Thought is not contrived or controlled. It's a free emanation of the mind. This must happen in a natural, comfortable way. The movements in the world will not soften until thought becomes clear and of a higher spectrum.

CHAPTER EIGHT

Changing Your Spiritual Mindset

The movement of humankind must be inward to open the recesses of the heart, for this opens the ways for exterior miracles to occur. To change the inward soul to greatness makes no demands for outward expression, but the carriage is different, the demeanor carries authority, and the voice holds both tenderness and strength. The mind knows when to speak and what to say and what not to say, and the heart encompasses a deeper, fuller resonance.

The soul develops through the thought, the awareness of God, and the desire to be a better person. The entire persona changes. The soul becomes ready to meet the God to say, "I have grown." The world waits for your soul, heart, and mind to be unveiled in God's glory. This is the moment wherein the beauty of your soul — the luminosity of your being — shines for all in the heavens to see.

Righteous people need not hide their souls from the world, for they are truth. Adorn no malice, gossipy tales, or mocking condemnation, for these are traits of people with weakness of the heart. Let every word, movement, act, or thought reveal the goodness of you, the wonder of you. A person of laughter, love, and joyousness resides in you.

Begin by monitoring the utterances from the mouth. Hold everything not in accordance with the new you. Go higher in thought, stronger in action, greater in words, and deeper in feeling. You need not be an audience in your life. Be the movement toward greatness. Ask God for compassion, for kindness, for love, for any quality of the heart that you need and desire. These will be given!

Build these in yourself. You are creating your most wonderful self.

The works of God are not to be diminished. God's creation is you. He has endowed you with freedom to develop the soul to the highest or to cower in no growth. Lift to God. Lift the heart of the soul to all the wonderment. Become the most worthy soul of which you are capable.

This life is to be cherished with every breath. This life is a gift from God. At the beginning of the life in the heavens when the soul readies to meet God, you give God the gift of the most wonderful soul you have become. There, you filled your heart with attributes that you carry through eternity. If you have dared to open the tender, vulnerable heart to feel love and compassion, you have employed courage of the most high.

You must grow to be the best person you are capable of being. This cannot wait while the people of Earth continue to wallow in ignorance. Stand up and let the world know you have risen from the darkness. Help humankind in whatever ways you desire. Raise the quality of thoughts in ways you desire. This must be an immediate action throughout the world.

Be a Person of Greatness

Now is the time to teach the souls of Earth the great ways of the gods and the angels. The world must learn these ways at this time because many changes are now due on Earth. People must be prepared to handle these changes with courage. The ways before were slowed and not globally effective. This is a small, unsophisticated planet with wars and harmful ways. Earth cannot go on in ignorance of the heavens.

People must know the worth of their actions. Words and thoughts affect the entire world. It's time for people to mature in their lives and become whole, intelligent, compassionate beings. This must be done now! Whatever your individual problems are, put them behind you, and think about the greater world problems. All things are ready and in place to change the world. People of quality must be ready to meet the new world challenges.

Don't be afraid to stand alone in your beliefs. Be strong and unafraid, and bend to no person or order that is not right for your soul. People of greatness will soon walk Earth. Angels will walk with them. These men will change the world. Be with them. Each person, each soul of Earth, has the possibility within to be of greatness.

Determine what you would decipher as great. Be this. Don't wait or waver. Be all you are meant to be. Do this now! Whatever you settled for in the past is not important. You are a person of greatness now. Be this person of power, wisdom, humor, compassion, strength, courage, and love. This is you from this moment through eternity.

Weakness is no longer a part of you. Subservient actions are not part of you. Illness and fear are not part of you. Ignorance is not part of you. Be the person God created you to be. Take on goals greater than your own prosperity or your own happiness. Be the mender of all humankind. Lift all humankind to happiness and to greatness. Honor God, for he is the center of you and of all that exists.

Use the Mind for Soul Growth

We are now asking the people of Earth to begin the move to acquire mental functions. Use the mind to develop the growth of the soul. The development is obtained by reasoning as well as the emotion in the human body.

Be the one who leads the souls of Earth. Use your intellect wisely. While in a human body, the soul experiences growth of either great movement or not much movement. Choose whether you wish to move toward God. Give your heart to love, whether that is one person or many. A person does not only lift to God but also can choose to grow enormously in this life on Earth. God issued your birth on Earth so that you might grow in the soul into enlightenment or grow toward the elevation of the spirit.

Be alive. By this, we mean live each moment. Experience life with fresh eyes. Be the most alive you can through all experiences possible. Live each moment in fullness. Let each day be new and full of life. The most wonderful life can be lived in joy and wonder if the mind is free and open to experience all life.

The people of Earth are to be lifted to a higher state of existence. Integration of the heart, soul, and mind are necessary to lift human consciousness to a higher state. As you grow, reality is experienced. Aliveness is experienced. The soul grows toward deeper and more fulfilling experiences.

Wonder is within each soul's grasp not by living within human regulations but by help from the heavens. Ask God to release you from ignorance and from fear of past actions. God is merciful to those who ask with a humble heart. The workings of God are not always understood on Earth. Let us teach the words of the gods. Be of good cheer. Celebrate the day. Let this day be one of joy and laughter. Let not work nor any person diminish the aliveness within your mind. Do your daily routine with the joy within and know it is a necessary way to function for movement in the world. Let it be done with a heart full of life.

Change Direction

Thought is more important than you can ever imagine. It is not only urgent to change thought but also the words you speak. It's easy and convenient to mock, to criticize, and to say foolish things to invoke a laugh from fellow listeners. But is that why you are on this Earth?

Laughter is wonderful! It's the voice of the gods, but the gods are already immersed in perfection. On Earth, the perfection is only in the deep soul, not integrated with the human mind. Cheerfulness will be a natural part of humanity as they grow in mind functions.

Now the mind and heart progress toward God. The mind will propel thoughts of a higher and nobler origin. Attributes of the heart will be integrated into mind function. The quality of thought will lift as you progress toward seeking God. Lower, coarse, guttural words and thoughts will become repugnant to the soul. As you grow before God, the natural movement will be that higher values will come to the mind.

This is not only a wonderful movement for humanity but it's also essential for the preservation of the world. If the populous of the world fails to realize that the movement of higher thought must be accelerated, the human species could fail to exist on Earth. The ignorant, lowly thought needs to change at this point. Should the world continue to regress into wars, suffering, ignorance, fear, greed, and the lower avarices, people will descend to undesired levels.

As people discard the gift of the world of Earth, will they contaminate other worlds?

Other worlds are higher than Earth: cleaner, purer, more artfully developed. Humankind would not be easily integrated into the more holy worlds.

The time has passed for humanity to change the destructive ways and progress Earth into enlightenment. We angels now plead with humanity to stop the morbid thoughts and the ignorant, selfish behaviors. These are the traits of an unruly child. To gravitate toward others, you must put away these behaviors, actions, and words to become truly great within. The world at this time needs to propel forward with intense exaggeration. From this moment, it's up to each soul to think, speak, and behave in a manner of God's viewing. It's not acceptable now to behave as unruly children. People must shed these traits unworthy of the self.

Has there been no acceleration of the soul's growth for eons on Earth? Have people learned nothing over time? Humans still gravitate toward power, money, greed, and material goods. People must now bring to the world the best of themselves; they must ask God for values of the heart and mind.

People of goodness can move Earth forward into graciousness, intelligence, and kindness. A world must evolve to these qualities to steady and grow — not only to maintain, but also to stop the movement of destruction and decline. Change begins with each person.

Unveil Your Luminous Soul

One day, people will realize the purpose of living in this world. They will step out of their limited views to see a wider, fuller existence. People will recognize living here is not a folly but a responsibility. Each soul has a responsibility to humankind and to God: This is to evolve your own soul, to become the highest and best person you can be, to help others in whatever way you can, and to grow toward God.

Should these not be realized by the souls of Earth, a time will come when all souls will cry out to God for mercy. The hatred must stop. The entire progression of humanity is not to wither and die but rather to flourish. If you are going home and the thought arises that you should be going in the opposite direction, do you not change the direction to move in the correct way? Using the same logic, when you look at the world's progression, you can deduce that humankind is moving in the wrong direction.

It takes one soul to stop, decipher, and change course. This is you! Look beyond your own greed and pettiness. Look to the evolution of the world. You, by changing your quality of thought, can affect the entire world! You are the one who must begin within yourself. One day, people will know the power the soul possesses. From this day forward, begin unveiling your luminous soul to the world. You are a soul of greatness!

Give no thought to possessions, wealth, power, or status. This greatness comes from exerting energy to comfort, serve, and help. This comes from obtaining the qualities of the soul. Tenderness, love, compassion, kindness — these are what will change the world!

As the world begins a cycle of new spirituality, people will notice changes more and more until wonders unfold. This is the choice of each soul. Why should Earth be as one of the hells? Why can it not be as one of the heavens? People must realize their own worth. They need to know they are creations of God and, as such, have an obligation to become the greatest souls possible!

Exterior wonders will manifest because the new movement of spirituality has begun on Earth. The word of God is now given and received.

It Takes Only a Moment to Change Your Life

How can we change our lives in a practical way?

Love and thought on Earth must be lifted to a higher quality. This must be done at this time in the movement of Earth. Each soul is to look within his or her own thoughts. If the thoughts are jealous, angry, or sad, the empty visions must be changed into thoughts of mercy, love, compassion, giving, and blessing. Don't allow the lowly, angry, or fearful thoughts to stay in the mind, because these thoughts manifest into what will happen in your life. Any moments left on Earth should be lived in joy, not in sorrow or anger. Why live these moments in proclaimed misery?

Adverse occurrences will happen in life. Pay close attention to the ways to respond. You can make a situation worse or enhance the moment through your response. Choose to make the moment better. Lift yourself out of the nucleus of the situation physically, mentally, and emotionally.

Grudges are not to be harbored. Let go and not only forgive ignorances and weaknesses in others but also send blessings to them with your thoughts, as they are most needy. Should people do harm to you, respond by blessing them and sending love through strong thought. Wonders can occur from this action. You can truly change your life through these actions, as you will be changing your trained ways of thinking.

You are cherished by God and God's angels. We see your shining soul. We know the power within you to do goodness in the world. When this is realized in the self, miraculous wonders will occur. This all begins with a thought. Envision what you desire to occur, for those who plan and can see their futures have greater focus to bring that desire into fruitation.

When we speak of "lifting" thought, we mean evaluating your thoughts. If you find yourself in an angry thought, in frightened thought, in painful thought, or in jealous thought, stop this way of thinking at once!

In a moment, Earth's consciousness could change. In a moment, the world could change for better or for worse. It's necessary for all minds that are open to practice these techniques. To do so will indeed change the entire world. Send thoughts of peace, love, contentment, and abundance. This will be acknowledged by the souls in the world.

You have the power to do this! Step away from the situation and understand that something more wonderful is in store for you, perhaps in a completely different venue.

Can you forgive those who have done harm to you? Yes, this can be done. Understand why people hurt you. A person might have caused you harm because of ignorance, selfishness, pain, or confusion. Be better than you have in the past in your reactions. Bless others and pray for them. Give compassion and understanding. If this particular situation of life is not for you, know the correct path is now open.

We are trying to help people look into their souls. This is what is needed to be one with God. Open the heart to be your true soul. Give this to others with love. When souls give away their money, material goods, and most precious possessions for the good of others, they walk barefoot to the Lord God. These souls are of enormous worth.

CHAPTER NINE

A New Look at Old Religion

Humanity is to endeavor to bring to the self the endorsement of the holy laws. The soul's intellect and heart knows what is right. The soul should not hurt or cause pain to another soul. Inflict no injury— not even in the mind — on another.

The soul is neither to thieve nor to desire the belongings of another but to bring glory to itself. Give not into the temptations of the wanton soul, for to do so may bring discomfort to others. Seek to help others in any way to bring life, glory, joy, or substance to any other soul.

The laws of the God are few but are of worth in bringing souls to God. Live in kindliness to make the choices to perform correct actions, think correct thoughts, and speak correct words according to the soul within. You are part of God.

Exercise Tolerance

How will the words of angels change religion?

The way that the religions will end is that the new truths will be understood and will not be in agreement with the old dogmas. The religions of the world will stand against the new truths of the angels. The angels will fill human minds and answer questions with truths not before given. When this occurs, the religions will fight to keep their practitioners. The young people will rebel against the old ways. Many who have worshiped in the old ways will be torn between what they believe and what they have seen to be true.

This will cause great turmoil in the religions. Many will begin to question their faiths. Others, with a deep love for God, will continue their paths to heaven. A deep servitude to God is a path to heaven. The young must not force the religions away from the elders. Let each soul find God in its own way. There will be a light of spiritual learning on Earth.

Some religions will try to add these truths to their sermons. People will seek God through their own souls rather than through a meeting place. The most important way to serve God will be to love God and others as you love yourself. Be with those who cannot understand and love them as they are now. Each path leads the soul to God. Respect each way to God. We angels will try to guide and help each soul.

Will these teachings negate previous teachings?

No one can know the entire truth of the heavens, but some religions provide much that is true about the heavens. These words will give you the entire look at the ways of God. We are the truth and the light. We give you words of truth. You can choose to understand or look away. This is the choice of the soul.

Words such as these are not to be bandied about as if they are words of fallacy, for they are not. These sacred writings are a gift to the souls of Earth. Merge them into your thoughts and deeds. Know them, as they will bring you closer to God. The ways of humankind can and will be altered. Which souls enter the new worlds will depend on the alteration of the behavior of these earthbound souls. We angels note the moments you spend communicating with God. We hear the pleas. We know the sincerity of the heart. We feel and watch.

Make no mistake, the religions of the world contain truths to help humankind, even now after centuries of mistaken interpretations. Make no mistake, the ways are not seen clearly. The most honorable people can misinterpret these writings.

Pray for Others

People who know God will serve him in ways not before done. There will be a spiritual awakening covering the entire world. People will seek God not only for solace but also as they pray for others. Most prayer is for the self. Now people will pray for others on Earth. People will lift their thoughts from hatred to help needy souls. We angels will rejoice at the growth of the soul. When the souls of Earth beg to help and pray to God with sincerity, we rush to the soul and surround that soul with love.

Why help others when we have our own problems?

When each soul is made a higher being, Earth will no longer be needed. It will become a utopia. Now poverty and disease permeate Earth. This can be changed. You are the catalyst who can generate the world. Ask God now to lift you from the ignorance surrounding you.

Be ready to change completely. Be ready to be open to new discussions. View life on Earth as the great gift it is. Let the gift of this life be given to you in all ways. If you have been a ghost of the world and only exist in hollow motions, let your eyes be opened now to bring joy to others. Experience this aliveness yourself, and it will radiate to others.

When your eyes are opened to see the good that you can achieve on Earth, the soul may gasp at the immense possibilities. A life once seen as integral will now see ways to help humanity. Begin by humbly asking God for assistance in achieving your goals. These goals will change as you are lifted to a higher perspective. When a soul can see the weeds of the world in the most essential views, it can reach out and effect change.

New experiences will open for you. New ideas will occur in the mind. Perceive all new ways. You should be a servant to God and not so involved in your own pain that you cannot see how to help others. Ask God how you can help others here on Earth. Ways will be given to you. You have the capability to change lives and to help make the world a more wonderful place to live.

Spiritual Law

Is baptism necessary to enter heaven?

The rites of baptism are not necessary to enter heaven or to be lifted to God. All souls are welcomed into God's domain. If a soul has not heard of God or of the heavens, it is lifted to God's love. No idolatry or religious practice is necessary, save prayer, to lift the pure souls to God. Lift from the ignorance of others' minds. Use your own mind. Think the thoughts for yourself. Curse God, and you will still be lifted to a place in God's heaven. God loves all of Earth with unconditional passion.

How important is confession?

People go to the papal office to tell of their sins, but each withholds secrets he or she dare not say aloud. Address these people and tell them the joy of letting go of all their burdens. Confess not to a papal authority but to God through prayer. When this is done, the soul will lighten and prepare to be lifted to a higher realm. When you hold the hard secrets and shamefulness inside, it is not as easy to lift to the higher realms of God.

When you know what is right and do not deviate from right action, wonders will occur for your soul. If a soul knows the right thoughts and actions but chooses to do other than these, that soul is bound by thought and action. Such a soul is heavy with the burdens of its own thoughts. When people give of themselves to others, they give the world their love and joy. People give from the basic goodness that is within themselves.

A soul is to confess only to God and to tell of all it no longer wants as a part of itself. A soul must ask God to remove the pain, the hate, the fears, and all that is not part of its perfection. The soul then begins a new life unburdened by sins of the past, unfettered by fears of being found out, and unmoved in its direction toward God. The one God is all forgiving and all generous to all who ask forgiveness.

The soul is made free by letting go of pain. This gives way for wonders to enter the soul. The contentment in unveiling your transgressions is a step toward the realization of God.

Is it possible for someone who has died to become an angel, god, or goddess?

We are appointed after many lives and many forms of existence. When someone on Earth dies in the body, much soul growth is needed to attain states of the organized heavenly positions. You must understand, Earth is the lowest of all the worlds. To leap beyond the heavens and beyond all worlds is not likely, but it is not impossible. The soul can perform many feats. The growth of the soul may take multiple lives. It may be open to much in the ways of growth.

Angels are appointed. Gods are appointed. An appointment is given the homage due the assignment. If all the ways the angels help those on Earth were known, you would bow to us and pay us homage constantly.

Church

Should I join a church?

Let the soul within lead you on the path to God. If you seek discipline or social conversation about God, a religion would serve you well. To lift your heart through song is a wonderful homage to God. To gather and proclaim devotion to God is a wonderful action.

You each have within you all knowledge and all remembrance of all things. You are all perfection in your souls. Listen to the voice of your own soul. You need not follow any doctrine made by humankind.

The relationship between you and God is completely personal and most sacred. The spirit and holiness of you and your God is the most wonderful merging. Follow your own religion and have your own knowledge, your own devotion, and your own oneness with God.

The rebirth of the soul is to be done in the quietness of the most sacred soul. This is a sacred communication between the human soul and the one God. This is to be conducted in private through the feelings of the heart. This is to be seen and felt by God alone.

In the aloneness of the soul, you may speak directly with God from the soul. No interferences surround the body and no performances are viewed. Only God and the soul are in audience with each other. This brings forth the openness of the heart to feel. The person may bring the depth of feelings to express only to God. The sincerity of the soul will be known by God.

Which religion has the true church?

The churches of Earth are all good in the way they keep God in sight of the practitioners. People reaching toward goodness in all the varied religions bring joy to all entities in the heavens. No church or religion is completely in tune with the heavenly realm. All are erroneous in some aspects.

The most significant and most pure religion is the church of women praying in unison for peace on Earth. This does not exist now but will in the future. The adoration of God will be part of every soul on Earth one day.

What do the angels think about churches having excommunication?

The religions giving this pronouncement do not understand the worth of the soul. The soul is a most honored, valuable being in God's kingdom. No action could keep the soul from entering God's heaven. The soul needs no more than the glorification of the self than to know it can speak with God through his holy angels.

People who have been excommunicated from any church or religion should know they are more than any doctrine or any ordinance made by human beings. They should stand tall in the knowledge that they are on a path to God. They need nothing and no one except their own devotion to God. Forgive the pain and sorrows of past mistakes.

CHAPTER TEN

Love and Soul Growth

What is love on Earth and in heaven?

Love is the tenderness of the soul meeting the mind and heart of the body and moving it into action. God loves as a person loves, only with a welding of love. When the heart fills with joy and desire, this is a worthy description.

The yearning for love is inherent in all souls. It's a natural feeling. This is a way to lead toward God. The love experienced by a human heart can be felt in many ways. The heart is not only a muscle in the body; it's also a culture of the soul. The more the heart wants meaningful love, the more it feels. The person not needing love is strong in the mind, but it is necessary for the heart to open, to be vulnerable, in order to feel the love surrounding you. The more the heart is open to feel not only love but also sorrow, the more compassionate you become.

We hope these words strengthen the mind, develop feelings in the heart, and lift the soul to experience the love surrounding the plane of the God-self. We are with each soul. On Earth, the love felt for another is muted because of the physical bodies, which are on a gross level. When you are in the heavens and no longer need a physical body, love is felt to its fullest.

True Love

When two souls who have loved deeply on Earth are together again, the ecstasy is overwhelming. Love is a thousand times more powerful than is felt on Earth. When love is felt this enormously on Earth, can you imagine how it will be in the heavens?

We will tell the story of two souls who did not marry each other. These souls married others because of miscommunication and circumstances but continued to feel deeply for each another. Neither could hurt the families they had raised or their spouses. They ached for each other, but nothing came of it. They remained in each other's thoughts and hearts, and when they died, they found each other in the same heaven. They were immensely happy to be together again. They were young again and free to experience love with each other. They are still in the heavens together.

This is a true story. Cultivate this feeling. Let love surround you. Love is so important. Let love be felt in many ways. Let love flow from your soul as if there is no end. Let it be free and wonderful. You are the love that is now your soul. Many on Earth yearn for this love, behaving as they were taught to, but not experiencing love as it was meant to be felt.

If you feel love for another soul, let it be known to the soul. Let that soul know the feelings in your heart because this love is a gift from God. Your life goes on forever. Let love permeate your thoughts from now into eternity. The way this is felt is not immediate. Realize that time has no meaning in the heavens. This love will be felt very intensely. This can be done for people you hold dear not only on Earth but also in the heavens. In the heavens, true love will emerge.

Love from before this life will be felt physically as a movement of the soul. When love is recognized, a trembling movement is felt. It's as a magnetic pull toward each other, unhampered by time or space. These souls have loved before and will be together through many lives on many worlds. Some will be together throughout eternity.

Love speaks of itself as honest and true, but it's evolved into an entity not understood, having features and powers. Love wants fulfillment of itself. It makes a mother cherish her child and a woman look at a weathered old man with desire and tenderness. It waits for nothing. It reaches into the depth of the human soul. It pulls to the mate until the heart aches, yearning to be with that soul. Opening to love now takes your heart and body into love — or whatever love portends. An energy merged in love, torrid and fleeting, lifts the soul into ecstasy and plunges the heart into despair. It never waits but to yearn for the two hearts melding into bliss.

In the heavens, you will have wisdom in all things and complete understanding of every feeling you experienced on Earth. You will know why you felt certain ways and why others felt and acted as they did. The wonder of this is that you are full of love when viewing this. Do not be too concerned with finding your true love. Many loves will come and go in life only to deepen the emotions. On Earth, it's more important to find a love counterpart. However, true love is now possible on Earth and in the heavens. There is a soul who is meant to be with you into eternity. Each soul is to progress into its individual growth and fullest potential.

You will attain the love you desire if this is what you want. Many choices are open to you. All the gods in the heavens are with you to help you make these decisions. If it's declared that you are to be with a love counterpart, it will be so. A love so intense, so deep, that a soul cannot be without this other soul is possible. This is a choice of the soul.

Thought is, at times, more important than deeds. What is not fulfilled will live forever in the mind to will it even more deeply. The desires fulfilled in a moment are fleeting. The experience is not savored as would be the desires a person waits many years to fulfill. A woman and man waiting to be together for a lifetime will emerge in all ways after this life.

Love is a way to receive joy in the soul. On Earth, all things are transient. On other worlds, souls are united into all eternity in a field of all love. It's different from what the people of Earth know. True marriage is known in other worlds. The soul is in varied levels of heaven. It loves at different depths. When a soul enters heaven, another soul may follow if this level of heaven is warranted.

Give Your Heart

What's the purpose of love?

The most valuable lesson a soul can learn on Earth is to love others. When you love another, the mind lifts to a level more expansive than when only loving yourself. This begins a love for humanity. A love for another human or a group of people opens the heart and mind to expansion. Only emotion can lift this feeling into an expression of love.

Give all that you are to another. We watch this unselfish act from the heavens. When you love and embrace others, the act generates feelings that lift the soul into pure bliss. On Earth, it may be painful, but in the heavens, it's bliss. Concern for others deepens the feelings and evolves the soul. This adds dimension to the soul. This lets the soul grow and expand into the same love experiences you feel in the heavens.

Love can be felt by all people. All souls know the feeling. Experience this love. Send this love to others. A love of the soul will be a love that shall endure all lives and all deaths.

How do we feel love?

This evasive word is as a social act with a varied depth of feelings. Love is a rising of emotion, a comforting togetherness, and an adoration of another being. Love is the act of treasuring the self when in the presence of a particular person. An absence of this in life creates the desire to feel this for another.

Love is a method of feeling God's adoration of all souls. This is a connection with God in all feeling — to feel love for others, to connect with them in words, thoughts, and feelings. Listen to them. Look into their eyes, cherish them, touch them, play, laugh, tease, and be in joy with your beloved. One day, you will reach for them, and they won't be there. Cherish every moment with those you love.

It isn't enough to just feel this love. It must be expressed. The touch of a hand can bring feelings from the soul. To enjoy the presence of another is a form of love. Take time to give of yourself to another, even if it is only to listen to that person's words. This means stepping back from your own thoughts and pursuits to feel what another soul feels. This is compassion, a gift of yourself to another.

Make time to connect and adore each other, to reflect how much a person's presence means in your life. Feeling deep appreciation, thankfulness, contentment, or joy to have someone in your life will come through in your words and actions. The soul will emit this brightness for all to see and feel.

Love is indeed a blessing, much like the bliss found in the heavens. These feelings bring a circle of attraction to you. The opening of your heart brings angels to your side. Let yourself feel love. This will bring the most wonderful events into your life.

How does the heart feel love?

We are so blissful in our lives of feelings. The angels communicate through the heart and mind of the soul. The wonders of God will fill the heart, and the consciousness grows. Those who open their hearts to feel the glories of God will also feel the pain of a gentle heart. They who have felt the pain of a loss and cried from the heart will love and feel joys unimaginable in the heavens.

We are so happy. We feel compassion in a deeper sense than you can imagine. It's not sadness but love. It's love on a much deeper level than you can experience, partially because of being in a body. Love is so important. Give your heart to love. The deepest love is the remembrance of heaven. Cultivate these feelings.

First feel contentment, then love. This is the glory of heaven on Earth. Even a dense body can respond to this love. When you look at a person, create the love inside you. Send it to that person. Thoughts of love for that person will be received. It may not be experienced on a level immediately felt, but it will be known. When you love with a full heart, this love is known.

How can we feel love practically?

We will now tell you of a way to cultivate the qualities of the heart. This is to be given to you to use daily. Sit and be still. Ask God to lift you from ignorance and fear. Let the angels surround you, and feel their love. Think of someone or something you are grateful to have in your life. To be thankful is to let the love of angels penetrate the culture of the heart. The soul within holds sweetness beyond expression. Giving sincere thanks lets you experience this sweetness. When the heart is full of thankfulness, it expands to fill with love not in physical size but in the heart of the soul. The soul holds both heart and mind. This is elusive of measurement, but it is in all souls.

The soul moves when the angels send thoughts of love to you. The eyelids may flicker as the physical body feels the presence. In some cases, tears may form. Some may be sheltered in light as if wrapped in a warm blanket. All these feelings are validations of angels around the body. The qualities of the heart may then be experienced in the mind. If cultivated daily, the qualities of the heart will be brought forth into daily activities. The qualities are kindness, love, compassion, sincerity, truth, joyfulness, cheerfulness, discrimination, intellect, wisdom, graciousness, and thankfulness. Your soul is brought forth. If it is possible, take time to commune with your surrounding angels. If the qualities of the heart are not utilized, you will become as a robot with no feelings, no emotions of love to draw on.

The soul is real. It is the you that is true, now and forever. Be the wonderful soul that is you. Cultivate the joyful qualities within the heart. This can be done regularly. It will help all aspects of your life. Nervousness, anger, and irritability will dissipate. This helps not only you but also all the world.

Experience you as you are meant to be by asking God and God's messengers to penetrate the heart in your soul. The most important way to be one with God is to pray to God with an innocent heart. By an "innocent heart," we mean without cajolement or without ulterior intentions. Be innocently asking without knowing the outcome to let it be God's domain. Ask with your clean thought. Let go of fears and animosity. Give only to God all that you are. Be God's child in all thoughts, words, and actions.

Relationships

Can you tell me about marriage on Earth and in heaven?

On Earth, love is real, but marriages are temporal. Marriage is a plan to weld together to help each other through this life. Marriage on Earth is not for the heavens. Go to the one God. Ask the one God. God loves all marriages on Earth and glorifies them. Love is final. When souls are united in the heavens, it's for all eternity. All the love one can hold will be directed to another soul in the heavens.

When the gods in the heavens sanctify the union, it will be with all the glories in the heavens. The soul is free to do as it wishes on Earth. Multiple marriages have no effect on the soul's growth. You may love more than one person and might also marry and divorce more than one person. Some realize the people they married are not their true loves. If the marriage is not dissipated on Earth, it will be of no concern after this life. A soul will be with the love it desires when in the heavens.

There is another soul who will be with you into eternity and has been with you before. You will know of this soul by the yearning to be loved by him or her and the trembling of your soul's movement when exposed to this person. In the heavens, when two souls have loved deeply and desire to be in marriage together throughout eternity, the sincerity and love is known by the one God and the surrounding holy angels of God. If this is given, the souls may dwell in heaven, to which their love ascends them.

This is God's gift to the beloved souls who love deeply and who give love to one another with all measure of devotion. Eternal marriages may be requested in the heavens. If they are given, it's because the love is strong and measurable. The one God looks into the heart to know the sincerity of the desire. When the world meets God, the loves meant to be together throughout eternity will be called united. We will welcome them into their eternal homes in heaven. We will let the world rejoice when the lifting comes to the souls. A marriage of true love will be reunited in the heavens. When this occurs, the most joyous love is felt. We await this as the joy echoes throughout the heavens. On Earth, other factors may be mistaken for love.

A word for those who cannot be together: Don't try to force unity in this life if it hurts anyone. When these souls enter heaven, those who love will be reunited. When lovers reunite, it's blissful beyond description. When a love is born in the heavens, the hope is to meet and marry on Earth. This does not always happen, but almost all wonders made in heaven are duplicated on Earth.

Do relationships such as marriage interfere with the soul's growth to God?

Marriage need not be a hindrance to obtaining grace from God. Feeling the obligations of a home, a spouse, and children may keep the soul from obtaining the infusion with the sacredness of God, but a marriage of contentment can enrich understanding in ways not explainable.

The complexities of the fullness of life can bring a thankfulness for joys you otherwise would not experience. To look at your children with thankfulness to God for the great gift of entrusting these souls in your care is a feeling of immeasurable joyousness. The soul will evolve as it should. The blessings of the Lord may contain the involvement with family life. Feel this love emerging from your soul. You may still grow in graciousness of the spirit. You may still hold tight to the sanctity of the holiness of God and give the most humble homage to the Lord.

What should we do when we are attracted to people other than our spouses?

All the movements without your love will be given back to you. All the love pent up inside you will be released in a flood of wonderment. A man loving one woman in the entire world of souls will be with her into eternity if the love is waiting to meet him. Lovers entered on Earth will be bound by desire. This desire will propel them to be with each other. One day, the world will be over. Use this time wisely. When two souls feel they should have been together but have married others, know that in the next life, all will be made right.

Is it necessary to cause harm to families and upheavals to situations in the name of love?

Mature people will wait until no one is hurt from their actions. Everything need not be done now. Your days will be endless. You will be able to do everything you dream. When the world meets God, the loves meant to be together throughout eternity will be united. We will welcome these souls into their eternal heaven. We will let the world rejoice when the lifting comes to all souls.

Souls uniting as one are two individuals merging together to behave in unison. They can dance and love as playful souls, and blend and swirl as lovers. Without a physical body, souls feel the purest, deepest love possible. Expression of this love may be in wonderful creations. All in the heavens love fully and joyously.

How do we know when a romantic love is the true love?

We want all souls to love. Feel the love in your heart. Desire to be with your beloved in every way. We want to perpetrate the soul's need for a relationship of the most wonderful. We allow the heart to feel greatness of emotion. The soul's yearning for true love is a growth needed on Earth. Love of this type is a wonder to behold. It should not be used to hurt another soul. Heaven waits for the different growths in humanity. Loves are measured by depth of feeling. The mirror of love is seen on Earth, but true love is known by the meeting in heaven.

When a soul falls in love at first sight, the certainty arises that these souls may have loved before. This is an enduring love. When the soul trembles from remembrance, it's a love from before this life. The sound of the voice is instantly recognized by the soul. It's the way people of greatness are recognized. Loves are shaken when they hear the voice and know the sound from before. A soul often marries a different person but may come across the soul love sometime in life. A way to know the true love is the feeling of trembling within.

Do we all have mates? If we don't find our true loves in this life, does this mean we have partners in the heavens?

Many are alone in this life and are lonely for someone they have not met. As the population increases, it becomes more difficult to connect with the true love. A person who has been alone the whole life may have a love now on Earth or may know love in the heavens.

Many can be a mate to bring contentment to the soul. The soul may not need another to be content. The soul needs to grow to God. This is the complete fulfillment the soul seeks. The ways may not be clear for this growth. People may need counterparts to help with the struggle of life. A soul's true love may be waiting in the heavens or may pass through this life.

A self-contained person may gain strength and courage from aloneness. The world is a difficult place in which to exist. A mate can help the difficulties become easier. Think not about your loneliness. Think of building a strong soul of courage and wisdom. Prepare the abode for the visitation of angels. Prepare the mind for wonders to occur in the life. Ready the body, the soul, the mind, the emotions, and the surroundings for the wonders. Help others by extending kindness and friendliness.

Wait with patience and know the mentions will occur. Build the wonders in the soul. Use this time to build the strong thoughts to seek fulfillments. Know the situation is a temporal movement in the life. The wonders will occur as you expect and dictate.

Loved and Lost

What would you tell someone with a broken heart?

We would tell you how to recover from the pain of welding your heart with another and being rejected. Know that the welding is of not much merit if it could not last and give comfort. If either fear or pain was in the merger, it was not a comfortable welding. If the plan set out by you and the angels (before you were born on Earth) was not kept, confusion will follow. This will be fine in one way because life will go on forever. Pain and sorrow may occur, but know that it is temporal. Know the strength within you will propel you into the next phase of your life. Your soul's desires will be fulfilled.

The knowledge of the life plan may not be known. The reason the merger dissolved may not be known until the body and soul separate at the time of death. All understanding will be known at that time. Now you must heal. Let your mind rest and heal. We angels know your feelings and will comfort you. Be still and know we are with you.

It isn't your main purpose in life to be with another soul. The purpose of your life is to evolve the soul. Think of your growth. If circumstances and separations are part of this growth, face these trials with dignity and courage. Losing a love is a deep sorrow and difficult to understand. When this pain is felt in the heart, it's as if the heart were breaking. This is not the case, but the soul is exposed and open to the pain. The way to understand the most tearful pain of a lost love is to know the reason is for your life to go in another direction.

Often this is not comprehended until the life on Earth is finished. Let yourself feel the pain and let the tears flow until you are no longer in pain. If the mind could know the life ahead and the true life after life on Earth, it would unveil that the future is so much more than you can imagine right now. The life ahead will be wonderful if you so desire.

Love was a wonderful chapter in your life that is now finished, but you have many other chapters ahead of you. A most interesting notion about being a soul on Earth is that you are with other souls who are as needy as you are. The wonder of this is that you can help each other. The way this is achieved is thusly: The person who can lift him- or herself out of sadness can also lift others. The most powerful way to achieve this is to understand that God and the angels surround you. A merger is done by listening and understanding. The soul can ask God for help in lifting itself and other souls. This is not a lifting of the soul after death. This is a lifting of the mind and soul during life on Earth.

The many who are in pain and despondency who will be moved to rise to God will need to do this. Close the eyes. Ask God to help you become as one with him. The understanding will be given from the heavens. This will occur. The you who is God's child will emerge, and the sins of the past will be absolved.

What would you tell those who lost their spouses through death and don't want to go on alone?

The way the heart yearns is a way to elicit desires. When love is the desire, the heart is made aware, even when apart from the connecting soul. When we love, it's not ended because we are separated by distance, death, or decades of time. Love your life now. You will reunite in heaven. When you are lucky enough to be on Earth in a human body, cherish the moments of joy and value the moments of growth. Wisdom and love are the results of a life well spent. Wonderment of the heavens and Earth will always occur in the secret moments of repose. On this Earth is where you should be now.

When the time to lift to heaven occurs, you will understand the moments of sorrow, the days of work, and the months of seemingly not going forward. When you are in a human body, you have a chance to reach to God. When the heart aches in love and is born in this life to fulfill it but the love is hindered by distance, time, or circumstances, the time will come when these souls will rise to the heavenly plane and be together into eternity.

One day, the souls shall reunite, and all shall delight as they enter heaven. The desire to love and be loved by another is so strong that when these souls enter heaven, it will be fulfilled as if the love were created in the heavens.

Let's say, over the period of a lifetime, a person has loved two or three people differently but equally. Do they end up with one of them after death, and if so, which one?

The spouse on Earth is not bound in any way to another in the heavens. When a body dies and has loved well, the love is retained after death. The soul is not bound to another soul except by want. If souls desire to be together, this will be done as desired. There is no moral obligation because the life on Earth was shared. Many lives will be known. In those lives, many loves will be recovered, each joyous in remembrance. The soul sees and understands all lives, not just the life on Earth. The loves of a soul will always be. You need not choose one over another. The heart of the soul will know the true love in the heavens. The soul may want only to seek God. All will be as it should, and the life in heaven will be in all perfection. No turmoil or jealousy will be known as on Earth.

The correct ways of all endeavors will be known. The soul views all possibilities and all the past in all lives. The soul understands from a perspective that is different from what is viewed from this one life. Many changes can occur. The soul's desires can change dramatically.

Love of a soul will continue after death. Many influences can change the direction of the soul's path. Many ways will be opened to the soul. When the life on Earth has ended, new possibilities will be opened. Your understanding will be that you will know the correct path for your eternal soul. The soul may wait many lifetimes or may choose in a moment.

Sending Love

How do we generate love when we're despondent?

The soul's true desires are heard when you show love instead of selfishness. Wonderment is now born. The love you will be experiencing will be a wonderful thing. The growth of love is the wonderment of the heavens. You will be the individual you are meant to be when you love. The experience of joy will lead you to God and you will become as a god under the one Lord God. The love will overwhelm you, and your plan in the universe is to be your will. You will grow and become as a god.

In a sorrowful mind lowly in thoughts, no light of God can be received. A mind must give way to even one thought of hope or love to be given the wonders of heaven. Ask the angels around you for help. The help will be given. Be not afraid to be met with the lifting arms of love. There is a need to feel love instead of empty words to placate a companion. To generate love, reach deep into your heart. Tenderness, compassion, goodness, kindness, and empathy are all within you. Ask for the highest entity around you, the one who appoints you to weld with you.

An angel may not appear to you physically but may send feelings of love to you. Be silent and aware.

How do we send love?

Feel the tenderness around you. To feel this in your own heart, devotion to God and intense gratitude will unveil this feeling. Make the love in your heart call to the world. When you express love to all the world, you are with God.

Give care to your thoughts and words, for they are true creations. They are not meaningless. Send blessings to each person you see through thought. Give words as gifts to the world. We walk with God, who chooses most carefully the mention of our thoughts.

When love is felt in your mind and soul, go to the sorrowful. Think and send overflowing love into their weak hearts. Give love until it's emptied from your heart. Create love and send this to the world. When you feel people's sorrow come into your heart, God will fill your heart with compassion.

You will know the wonders of God when the pains are lifted from your bodies. God, the Father, will work through your love to weld into the hearts of others. The soul is tender and delicate. Let yourself feel the opening of the soul. Bring this into your daily living. When you bring forth any of these emotions and feel this, it sustains longer. Think of anything you cherish, and feel deep love, profound gratitude, awe, genuine joy, and immense emotion. Feel as if at any moment you would break into tears from love and compassion. Most shelter themselves from these feelings. This tenderness is a part of your soul. Bring it forth.

Feelings are the true language of God. When the lifting comes, this will be known. These feelings can change the ways you react to life and enable you to view situations with merciful compassion.

Cultivate these feelings to soften your demeanor. The eyes will soften. The voice has a gentleness. An inner peace floods your consciousness. Open your heart to vulnerability to create wonders in the life. The movement of the soul's heart within the human body is an awareness of living in the soul rather than the body. This is truly being yourself. This is discovering your soul. Tears may form when opening the heart to love. This opening is a way to experience God on Earth.

It is during the most triumphant moments of humankind that souls open to feelings. The thoughts, words, and actions come from the comprehension of these feelings in the soul. Let the actions in the world be from the souls, not from repetitious, unfelt thought. When your heart is open and you are aware of the angels' presence around you, you are in a powerful position to accomplish magnificence in the world.

You would think a barrier of no feeling would be protective, but it's not true. Feelings with an open heart and soul bring forth armies of angels. Strength is multiplied. The way love is sent forth is by lifting thought and feeling God. This is done with the opening of the soul. Feeling gratitude for anything or all things will open the heart. Feeling genuine love for anyone vibrates the soul. Feel compassion and sincerely want to help others. Feel awe for life, for God — for anything.

One method of sending love is to generate the feeling of love in your heart. Ask God to help you feel this love and compassion at this moment. An angel will be with you to grant you these requests. Let the love inside you build in thankfulness, empathy, and praise for God and God's angels. This love can be generated by feeling deep, strong thankfulness and gratitude.

When the movement of the soul stirs within the body, it's a movement toward the planned lifting. An opening of the soul's heart is to be a wondrous feeling. Be thankful for any wonder on Earth, and the heart will feel the tenderness expand. This is the way the soul may begin to experience God. Once this is felt, the rejection of God is difficult. To be vulnerable to the pains of life is to open the heart. Pain may enter, but love and tenderness will enter as well. Let yourself be open to all the emotions of the heart. People of great strength and power try to shut out these emotions, but even if opened in solitude, they will help lift the soul to God.

How do feelings and emotions fit into this?

The more the heart wants meaning and love, the more the heart feels. Love is a way to lead to God. The love felt by the human heart and soul can be so intense that it will be emulated in the heavens. The human heart can feel in many ways. The essence of the soul might be so intense that tears could form in the physical body.

Physical responses such as gasping, fainting, and crying are all reactions from emotions. Feelings are the way many souls communicate. These are expressed by thought, actions, and emotions sent forth. Love is felt in the strongest intensity and is given to God or other beings. This is to be cherished. When compassion comes forward, the body responds. Love comes forth in a wave. The physical body stirs with the movement of the soul's heart. The angels watch and feel love when it occurs. To generate this, let tenderness open the heart to feeling. The love will be pronounced.

If we can send blessings and love to anyone, why can't we send this to God and the angels?

The thoughts, prayers, love, and blessings that lift the loved ones in the heavens and help those on Earth will also lift to God in his highest heaven to even more happiness. Writings on Earth have told you to give to others as you would want to receive. This is meant not only for people of Earth but also for those in heaven.

You can exult yourself to give blessings, as many blessings have been given you. Lift yourself to bless God and all the heavens as well as all around you. Give no distinction whether this be toward a friend or an enemy. Bless everyone. God and the angels of God will exult in feeling this from a mortal being. This will give a flood of joy to the recipient. Send blessings with a most sincere heart. You are worthy to bless as a child of God on Earth. There is no end to the love within your soul. The more that love is sent, the more it is replenished. Let your love shine to all the world.

Heaven on Earth

Love and kindness cannot be separated. Love and kindness are to be integrated into each soul. When kindness and empathy are part of your demeanor, souls step back to view this. Not even one soul can turn away from kindness. This is the way to bind the hearts of humankind. If a soul is to stand alone in this, let it be, for the lowly souls will take notice. Souls emit love in the higher levels. This is visible to all entities, as the soul is encompassed in light.

The heaviness of the human body, the thoughts of demise in Earth's atmosphere, and the low emanations from the people's souls contribute to the inability of the soul to feel love on Earth. Humankind must lift the quality of thought to the highest level they are capable. As this filters through the atmosphere of Earth's realm, the capacity for souls to feel and spread love on this world will occur.

A soul who prays to God for desires has experienced the method for sending strong thought. Now the soul can send the thought of love and happiness to others on Earth. As this is done, the world will be immersed in love, not in hate. Now Earth is wallowing in ignorance and self-gratification. This must change. It's not enough to do a few deeds of goodness, to be amiable, or to listen to clergy one day a week. Each soul must let go of animosities and bless all perceived enemies. Each must ask the angels for help to receive strength of character and fulfillment beyond the self.

The human mind is meant to send thoughts of love. If it be for only one soul, this in unison will bring the power of infinite and eternal love to the lowly world. Love will multiply, emerging as an ocean, which is the essence of the one God. This is to be the goal of every soul on Earth, not to live in fear or hatred but to send love with strong, unwavering thought to all souls, to every living being, to God, and to all entities of the heavens. What wonders will occur on Earth!

When souls not only forgive those who have done harm to him but also sends loving blessings to their enemies, they have chosen the ways of God and of the heavens. As this multiplies, Earth shall become as a heaven. When you look at a loved one, send love with strong thought. Do not think your mind cannot change the world, for this is in error. The thoughts and feelings from one soul can work miracles.

Earth carries the thought, the creations, and the inventions. The feelings of all inhabitants of Earth — the apathy, depression, pains, and suffering of all souls — carry in the ethers to bring joy to a mundane low level. The souls of Earth are hampered by the feelings and low thoughts over the world. This must be changed. The thoughts must elevate. The feelings born in the individual souls must ascend to incorporate joy, love, and happiness.

Do not wallow in despondency. Lift to give love to another. Feel love for anyone. Lift the thought. Let go of any memory of the past that brings you to a lowly mind. The soul has grown into a value of the human body, not meant to ever feel lowly or demeaned. Lift to the highest potential you can possibly maintain, for you are a creation of the one God. The purpose of your life on this Earth is to grow to God in all ways. This life is short, and eternal life with God's mentions is forever.

CHAPTER ELEVEN

Communicating with Deceased Loved Ones

We want to tell you how to mend ways with those who are no longer on Earth: Require their presence. Ask the angels to bring them to you. When they are in the room with you, tell them of your feelings. They will hear and respond. You may feel the spirit respond by surrounding you with feelings of peace and love. They will communicate with you to convey their feelings. They will understand your thoughts, words, and feelings.

Do not think because they are no longer on Earth that they do not hear you. The knowledge is that each soul is eternal and will make known all feelings, all thought. Let everyone of the world know that the people who have lifted to the heavens are more alive there than they were on Earth.

Visiting with Loved Ones Who Have Died

Do the recently deceased visit people on Earth?

Yes, many return or communicate from the heavens or the opening of the heavens. They are fully aware of the lives they left behind and their loved ones on Earth. They complete the lifting with the angels and discuss that they want to make sure all is well with those left behind on Earth. This is given as requested.

Some may call from the heavens as a phone call to the soul. Some may come to Earth in spirit to help a loved one, or some might whisper to those on Earth. This is only temporal. When they want to return to the heavens, they request this from the angels.

Children who have lost parents may be aware of their presence and will want to communicate with them to keep them here. This is not wise, as the soul has many duties to accomplish in the heavens. You may cherish those who have died and send them loving thoughts. But do not try to hold them to Earth.

Even after souls have resided in the heavens for a long time, they may come back to look at their children or loved ones. This is to watch over them. They may be seen or not seen, heard or not heard. They know of occurrences that are about to happen in their loved ones' lives and might want to comfort, give warning, or tell of a wonder.

Don't be afraid, for they cannot harm you. They are with you only to help as one of God's heavenly beings. When anyone in the universe is wanted, just ask for the person, and that person will hear your thoughts. Request the wonders you need for others, and if it is to be, it will come to you. Heaven is the answer to all prayers.

The wonders of God are more enlivening for the soul than anything you can capture in the imagination. The only way a person sees the world is through his or her own perspective. This is natural, but if a person stepped out of that viewpoint to encompass things from all angles and all sides of a question, he or she would be replicating heaven. One day this will be known.

After a Person Dies

After death, does the soul stay on Earth for a time?

Some souls wait until the funeral is over and the loved ones are past the initial grief. You may lift immediately with the angels or request to stay with loved ones for a short time. If your loved ones are far from where the body dies, you might travel to see them and try to communicate.

People tend to view their lives on this Earth plane as their only existence. This is an introduction to a myriad of lives that are before you. Wonders will occur that will stimulate you to greater aliveness and joys. Don't fear death. This will come to all. This is only a beginning to wonders beyond earthly comprehension.

When the death of the body occurs, the soul (which is you) will open to feel light and joy. Celebrate the end of this life, for it is the beginning of eternal bliss. God will come to you through the angels to lift your soul. Can you in your most sacred thoughts imagine this miracle? Worlds upon worlds know of these wonders, yet those of Earth remain in darkness.

How long is it after a soul enters heaven that the soul is still aware of earthly things, or is it at all?

Remembrance of the past life exists, but they are only glimpses of loved ones at varied times. Souls can come to Earth to see loved ones or to give messages, but their lives are now in the heavenly realm. They have much to do in the heavens. They no longer dwell on the Earth plane. They no longer desire to live in the past. The souls live in the heavens but know of the lives they lived on Earth. They make inquires of angels or of souls of Earth, but they are not earthbound. Their lives on Earth are over. Love for a child or a romantic partner might keep them aware of Earth for a while.

Souls want to begin their new lives in the heavens without encumbrances. When they are received in the heavens and they have questions about things of Earth, they contact the Men of Decision for help. The Men of Decision help relate any necessary communications between the lifted soul and any soul on Earth.

Why can't we communicate regularly, or sometimes at all, with those who have died?

When souls leave the body to enter heaven, many dimensions are opened to them. One of these is the body of Earth. Souls see those on Earth most clearly. Their needs are no longer of Earth, and they will focus attention in other areas. Souls seek to send messages to loved ones that "all is fine" because the earthbound can't understand the spectrum of the heavens.

How will people who have lost loved ones know they will meet them again?

The loves — and the souls bonded by hate as well — will be together again. When a person lifts to meet God, life on Earth seems to fall away. If you want to see another soul, you need only desire it.

How do deceased souls communicate?

The ways that deceased souls communicate are often visual, as in seeing them appear in actuality or in a dream state. They come to make known that the life will not end with the death of the body. Much communication can be done if the entity is seen before you.

Don't be afraid that they will take you. See them and speak with them as if they will hear and understand you. (We are speaking of souls who have lifted to the heavens, not lowly spirits who wander Earth.) The sighting will be sustained. A parent may come to visit a child on Earth. Angels are asked by the soul, and this is given. Angels may watch over the soul on Earth and the entity from the heavens. This is done most generously. We angels try to bring wonders to the souls.

The fear of death is prevalent when a soul from heaven or an angel is viewed. This is not to be indulged, as it is not an omen of death. Those on Earth can perceive many occurrences of varied dimension. These are not to be feared. The love supersedes all movements.

When a soul in heaven moves into purposes directed by God, the life on Earth becomes as a dream. Extreme love will bring the soul to Earth to know those left behind are safe and have accepted the death. The souls of Earth are to let them go into the heavens. Do not hold them to Earth or to you, for they have much to accomplish in the heavens.

Know that you will be with your loved ones again. The love will always remain. The memories can always be brought into focus. Their lives on Earth are done. It's time for them to begin their new lives in the heavens. When it's time for you to leave Earth, know you will reunite with them. This will be more wonderful than can be imagined.

Can we send love to deceased loved ones? How does this affect them?

Yes, oh yes! When you remember anything wonderful about them, communicate this feeling to the departed soul. This can be written and addressed to them, or you can ask your surrounding angels to convey the message to them. The angels will give the written or verbal message to them. If you ask forgiveness for something said to them, they will understand your feelings. Give love and blessings to them. They will feel the deep, sincere feelings of gratitude. They will be joyfully lifted in the heavens. This is a most wonderful thing to do for your loved ones.

A soul recalls loving attributes about the deceased. Direct the thought to the heavens. Know they will receive the message. One is not to try to keep the loved ones here after death but should send thoughts of love to them. A compliment on Earth will not be felt deeply because of the atmosphere, but as it's sent to a more subtle existence, it becomes more powerfully felt. Think of what a loving thought sent to God will inherit.

CHAPTER TWELVE

Begin the New You

The human body is given to the soul to be used as desired, but you should treat yourself with a high respect. This mortal body is not to be used as a lowly object. It's an honor to be in a human body. This is the clothing of your most sacred soul. The body is an expression of the soul and is to be used in a manner worthy of the self and of God.

Earth is now in a cycle of destruction. Prayer must be given from all over Earth. This prayer will help bring the world to the path toward goodness and completeness again. Heartfelt words given to God in a prayer of compassion for all humankind can enact miraculous changes in Earth's atmosphere, and wonders may occur in the world.

Heartfelt prayer to all humankind is necessary for the inhabitants of the Earth to do this now. This must be done! People praying for all humankind may change the future occurrences of the world. This is a wonder in itself — to lead all to prayer. But when the souls of Earth see the way it will change the movements occurring now on Earth, they will know of the power of their own thoughts and feelings. This will be done on Earth. This is ordained! Now is the time to teach the souls of Earth the great ways of the gods and the angels.

Many changes are now due on Earth. People must be prepared to handle them with courage. The previous ways were slowed and not globally affected. This is a small, unsophisticated planet with wars and many harmful ways. Earth cannot go on in ignorance of the heavens.

Be the Soul You're Meant to Be

People must know the worth of their actions. Words and thoughts on Earth affect the entire world. It's time for people of Earth to mature in their lives and become whole, intelligent, compassionate beings. This must be done now. You must grow to be the best people you are capable of being. This can't wait while the masses continue to wallow in ignorance. Help humanity in whatever ways you desire. Raise the quality of thought. This must be an immediate action throughout the world.

Whatever your individual problems have become, put them behind you and think of the greater world problems. All things are ready to change the world. People of quality must be ready to meet the new world challenges. Ask God for guidance to lift you out of your sicknesses and discomforts. It's time to become a better person. We angels are asking the people of Earth to be the souls you are meant to be. Realize that God and the angels are with you at every moment. Behave in a way worthy of this. This is an awareness of celestial entities at all times. We seek only to help you grow to God.

If you covet an item and no one would view the theft if you took it, would you steal it? If people were watching you steal the item, would you take it? If angels of God saw you steal the item, would you take it? To a person of goodness, the answer to all three questions would be the same. The idea of theft would not enter your mind.

Be a person of worth in your own eyes as well as those of your peers. Bring stature and honesty to your being. Stand alone, and know you are not capable of dishonor. Be truthful, for you are to be honorable to yourself. People of this greatness are glorified by the angels. Honors will be bestowed in the heavens.

Angels watch and know you have brought glory to them, for you are their charges on Earth. We angels rejoice at the growth of the souls on Earth! If a temptation comes to you and you repel it, we watch in wonderment. We are unseen and unheard to most so as to witness you becoming your most wonderful, and we watch with pride. Anytime you choose to help others over yourself, we see this. When you think and rebuke thoughts not of the highest, this is witnessed.

Perhaps you lived in a lowly heaven, and the experiences in a physical body on Earth were needed to lift you closer to God. Be a person of merit. Give no worth to lowly acts and words. You alone will stand before God. You alone will judge yourself with all knowledge.

You Are on Earth to Strengthen the Heart of the Soul

Is Earth just a place for unwanted souls?

No, this place (being the lowliest world) accepts all souls requesting a physical body and a birth on Earth. The souls of Earth are of varied interests and levels of growth. No one can say this world is only filled with unacceptable souls. This world consists of a myriad of diverse souls, each creating its own path through eternity.

These souls requested to be born in physical bodies on Earth. All things were discussed with the angels, and a basic life path was formed. Having no remembrance except instinct, the soul may deviate from what was preplanned. This is all due to the choices of the soul. The soul has complete freedom to move in any direction desired.

On Earth, the soul cannot generally perceive the one God or the entities of the heavens. The soul can perform any thought, word, or action desired. Life on Earth is one movement in all eternity. It's the beginning of the way to God.

Will we meet God in our thoughts as well as physically after this life?

Yes, the ways to meet God during your life are given, as in lifting your open heart to meet God. Make requests of God with sincere, genuine love in your heart. To receive audience, keep God always in the mind so that your actions are in harmony with the heavenly influences.

There is yearning for a love unexplained on Earth. Souls try to find this fulfillment of love in another soul only to be disappointed. This is an intense longing for the heavens and for God's love.

Are we on Earth supposed to know these truths after being born here?

No, the memory is in the soul, but until the mind and heart integrate and unify, the truths of the heavens will remain mysteries. You can look at the infinitesimal wonders of all creation and know of the intelligence.

Why don't we remember?

The world of Earth is in complete freedom and without interference from the gods and angels. Even acts of ignorance can be areas of growth. Freedom as desired by souls of Earth cannot be lived with knowledge and visibility of heavenly supervision.

The people of Earth are to will the forces to move toward God by developing qualities of the heart and mind. Now Earth is a world of little growth. This must change. May our words spur the movements in people's souls. Let these qualities into your being. If a few things of the life fall away, new, more wonderful occurrences will appear. Give no thought to losing what now exists, only what will exist in the soul.

You build your soul by strengthening the heart of the soul and the mind; this is what you will live on after this life on Earth. A world of only taking pleasures in things is not a movement toward God. The soul will move toward immediate happiness. The words of angels are meant to tell the people of Earth to live fully on Earth and lift your souls to God. Gravitate toward becoming of higher quality. Be a person of dignity and respectfulness, a person you would proudly show to God. As your heart soars, the love you sought is fulfilled.

A person's measure is not the goods acquired or the earthly powers sought and won; it is the strength and dignity he or she possesses of the soul. Angels watch and help you attain these measures. If you try but fail, we help lift you to try again. Ask us, and we will surround the soul with our strength. You always have our love beside you. You need only to be aware of our presence. Make no mistake, you are never alone. Tell us the achings of your hearts. We feel your emotions and will help in any ways possible. Any soul reaching out for us will be comforted. We cherish our charges on Earth and want all goodness for them.

When followers of God weld with the entities of God, the ways of the heavens are infused into their minds. End the pleas of woe. The light of God cannot enter where the soul is filled with despair. One day, the truths shall be practiced on Earth. When this occurs, the meaningful truths will endure over much time.

We angels of God applaud the souls brave enough to endure the salutations of hate given because of our words. Meet all against you with our words: Let this not be the only way to God, for many paths exist. Any religion or belief system saying it is the only true way to God has much to learn.

After this life, can we live in any world we want?

A life on Earth is only a steppingstone to a more glorified life in the heavens or in another world. Worlds sometimes don't accept specific souls. All are known by the energies emitted from the soul. Requests are made to enter the higher worlds. Should a soul not desire to make a request elsewhere, it can reside in the heavens.

Worlds upon worlds exist, all with the purpose of evolving souls. Some worlds are not suitable for every soul, so a soul might be directed to more comfortable worlds for it. A life of specific interests will gravitate to like inhabitants.

You in the New World

You are the most beautiful, luminous soul. Your life's purpose is to help humankind and grow toward God. To make any soul happier in any way is a growth toward God. Let your life be sprinkled with grace, love, tenderness, courage, strength, honor, fortitude, and compassion. Be this! Let the world see your highest and greatest worth! Behave and speak in a manner befitting a disciple of God. Treat everything in your life with the employment of these words.

Enter your home not with complaints but with loving joy. Let your surroundings radiate with this loving countenance. As your soul radiates and your surroundings glow with this love from the heavens, other souls will be drawn to your surroundings. Love and prosperity will flow to you. Give your love to all you encounter, be it through kindness, joy, compliments, greetings, sending thoughts of love, or good works. Imagine yourself as your absolute best. Work toward becoming this. Be this!

Your soul is all perfection. Be your soul! Wonders will begin to occur in this life. Miraculous events now have the possibility of occurring. Things will begin to happen that you never could have dreamed of!

Let go of feelings holding you to the lower levels. Lift yourself into the realms of all possibilities. Two actions must be taken to begin the new you: Rid the soul of all encumbrances and animosities, mental or physical, and stand alone as a soul created by God and beg him to lift you into the light.

This will be done. A selfless and sincere person can ask God for these wonders, and these will be given. God has placed before you all you have ever desired in the heart. All will be given to you.

Live your life in gratitude, not in complaint or condemnation. Live in bliss, even on the lowly Earth, by sending blessings and love to others. You hold the responsibility for your thoughts, your words, and your actions. Would you be one to thieve, gossip, complain, curse, or condemn if you knew your guardian angel were beside you this very moment?

Think Beyond Yourself

Can I have material possessions?

May no one want a material object, for use of this power of more and better happiness lies in service to others. For a person of greatness to bend to help someone in need is a more wonderful occurrence than the accumulation of all personal desires.

Humanity, the reason you are on Earth at this time is to help others. Spend little time in your own desires, for to help others will be counted in the next existence. The ways you cried in the soul for another and the ways you stopped thinking about your own happiness and gave of yourself for another's happiness will be known by all angels and all gods in the heavens. The world has worked toward self-gratification for centuries. Now is the time on Earth for you to move in a higher direction. Go beyond your own happiness. Give help where needed. Care for others from deep within your heart.

The time is over for competition for the largest, fanciest, newest, and best. From this time on, humanity must give feelings and thoughts of deepest reverence to God and feelings of love to even their enemies. When someone frustrating is in your presence, send your healing love to this person. One soul on Earth can't know all the problems other souls on Earth are holding. Earth is inhabited by souls who need love. A life of any soul needs your compassion.

The soul needs nothing in the face of God. The soul needs little on Earth, for simplicity brings the soul closer to God. This is not to be forced. The soul may be at a level wherein it needs physical manifestations. When the soul is given in complete devotion to God, things of Earth are meaningless.

As thoughts and feelings come into the mind, determine if they are good or bad. If it's determined that these are unwanted thoughts, change them immediately! Think of anything that brings happiness to the mind. As this is done continually, the mind will gravitate toward more positive thought and feeling in a natural way. Changes will begin to occur that ordinarily would not come about. Now, as you become more and more integrated with your soul, use this power to help others.

Become a Disciple of God

Words cannot express the ways we angels love our charges on Earth. Our love is unbounded, eternal, in fullness, and in celebration of your aliveness. We treasure you and cherish you in ways we can feel as we feel God. Not only will we love unconditionally, but we will also surrender this love to God.

When you are aware of the angels and all entities of the heavens around you, know the light of your soul is to be known at every moment. Meet this awareness with thankfulness, for all wonderment in life will open the soul's heart to God. A more intense aliveness cannot be felt in outward expression, for opening your heart to feel God is a more intense expression than any mortal can know. Can you be more in tune with God than to bare your soul in humbleness and ache that you might know of him? This is a true devotion, a rich, caring feeling from the deepest soul within. Be truly thankful, even if you own but little.

God is more than a symbol of highest intelligence. God is a living energy in the highest form in all eternity. God is here on Earth with you this moment. Feel God. Now, beginning with you at this moment, this aliveness is to be felt. This reverence is to be experienced. This is to be felt in the soul by you now! From this moment, you will change to be a disciple of God.

The homage you display is for you alone to view. No one is to view this, as it is a sacred connection between you and God. Audience would distract your purpose. The communication is now a sole viewing of you and unseen heavenly entities. Lift your heart to God to send him blessings and love. The moments spent in this communication will be held in your consciousness and will reflect in your completed demeanor. A tenderness will unveil to all. This will remain through all time.

When you can bless all encounters, you are holding the glory of the gods. Let the life unfold in its own time. Let the gifts be received as they are due you. Give the thought to benefit others as well as yourself. All things are not to be now. Some are to be received later. It's better to receive nothing now and receive what is to come to you at a later time because it will come without encumbrances. No barriers need be attached.

You will receive freely and completely if you do not demand it be given now. There will be no strain or torment connected with receiving these gifts.

Embrace the Wonders of Life on Earth

What if I don't care about this life on Earth?

Now you are on Earth. To only look to the heavens for comfort is not the planned way. Make this life on Earth as your heaven. Life on Earth is more precious than is imagined. The most significant life viewed by others might be the most powerful growth of any soul. Give no thought to the material, to possessions or clothing or food or an abode. All will be given in the heavens.

How does hate affect us?

When you hold a lifetime of bitterness, it will reflect in your health and demeanor. Not one Child of God is to hold hatred within. Forgive others the moment they let go of your attention. Make your life one of joy instead.

Hate and unwarranted stress affects the organs of the physical body in unhealthy ways. It's necessary to rid the body of these feelings, clearing your thoughts. Let go of any hate or anger, and bless others as you forgive them. Now the body can fill with feelings of health and love. Hate, fear, and sadness are all poisons you would not want in the body. Fill the body with love, tenderness, compassion, and peace.

How can we forgive?

Don't expect to lift to the angels from a deep hole of self-pity. You are now to begin a new life. You are only causing yourself pain by holding hate, resentment, fear, and animosity. Forget the past. Let every image of it be gone from your life. Ask your angels to help. The old feelings you're holding and letting harm you will be gone.

Forgive everyone in your past who has ever harmed you. Why, if you can choose your moods, would you choose to feel bad? You will realize understanding. Let all feelings of animosity lift, and the new you — free from hate — will emerge. This is the soul, the true self, before any hurt and pain. You are to go beyond the letting go of ill will. Bless this person so that the soul will feel the blessing. When this is done, much joy will come to you.

What's to keep anyone from using the powers of the mind to cause evil?

The consciousness of a human mind must be elevated to be able to enact change. An ignorant or distraught mind could not do this. A soul is to rise to a point where no sadness, no fear, and no anger can enter the mind. When the mind is full of love and fulfillment, the thought will be formed in a mind encompassed in loving thoughts.

Let us explain: Thought is germinated in the mind. It moves to an area of the brain where one can decipher whether to state it aloud or keep silent. This is a discriminating area of the brain. Not only can the mind determine if a thought is to be spoken or not spoken, but it can also decipher whether the value of the thought is to be discarded or remembered.

Any thought not worthy of being spoken aloud should be discarded. If self-effacing thoughts were discarded when they first come to the mind, many illnesses, diseases, or moods of depression could be averted. Many acts of violence could be ended before they come into realization. Before a thought is spoken aloud, ask yourself, "Is this a thought worthy for God or the holy angels to hear me speak? Are these words going to hurt or help humankind?" If you all watched words and actions more carefully, so many wonderful things would begin to occur on Earth.

The love and devotion given to God cannot be measured by humankind. God knows the feelings of the deep soul. To truly open the soul to God is to give all to him. This is true devotion. This is immeasurable. Any soul giving all in a love that is so unending will plan the life to reach to God. This ecstasy in the soul is the complete spectrum of feeling. Feel God touching your soul. This is more than a belief in God, more than a love of God. The souls of Earth are to hold God to them in all endeavors. Let God's graciousness touch every action. Let kindness become a part of you. You are the magnificent creation of God. Know this in every decision, every movement, and every thought. This is the most wonderful knowledge you can acquire to feel God.

The ways of humankind are to go through trials before they truly seek God in the highest parts of their souls. Many ways are given, but each soul must seek communication with God in a moment of quiet refrain. This is not through words or even thought but through feeling. God is feeling in all ways.

When the soul opens the way to feel God, all wonders are open to it. The soul cannot remain in a state of ignorance. If only for a second, it has found God. This is the true emersion into the one God. Do this not with an audience but in your aloneness. Let your heart speak to God. When this is done, angels flood to your side. We rejoice at the movement of feeling God. Soar with us in your soul. One day, you will know of us and of the gods in the heavens. This will be a glorious day. We bring all love to you as you bear your soul to God.

In the movement of the worlds, the generation of energies is in all worlds and in all heavens. Life takes many forms, spiritual and physical. The life force is given manifestation through the soul. Life in the most glorious sense is from the soul. Bringing this life forward into the body is now to be done. One must truly believe against all else that miraculous events can and do occur. The force of life energy is to be brought to the surface and felt in its entirety. This is a force of God's energy within each soul.

Experience the breath of life with each movement. Let God watch your every thought and action. Emerge now to the highest strength. Be the most wonderful being you are capable of becoming. Feel this within you. Greet each moment with an expectation of wonderment. Do not let the weariness or bitterness and sadness hold you from being the complete wonder you were born to be. The movements of God are everywhere. Believe in miracles. They will occur as you desire.

This moment is your moment. This day is your day. This now is the most wonderful day of your life. This moment is the planned wonder of your consciousness. In your next encounter, look, listen, feel, and care. A depth of feelings will emerge. Give attention to others. Be ready and prepared to receive the wonders in your life.

How do we prepare?

Make your abode and surroundings worthy of angelic and heavenly visitations. Prepare yourself. Calm the mind, but feel the excitement and anticipation of an angelic visitor coming to you. Make life as beautiful as possible this day. Give honor to all heavenly creatures, whether it be a god, an angel, or souls of the heavens. Give them the proper homage.

Mortals cannot often hear or see these figures. They will appear, but not all can perceive the light, the values, and the holiness of these entities. Prepare for any wonderment to occur. Address the entities of God in what you deem as appropriate attire. Rid uncouth thought from the mind as well as uncouth speech and action.

Expect miraculous events, for miracles will occur in as much depth as the intellect will allow. The love of God is to be felt in fullness. Let this come forward in humbleness before all who are greater than mortals. Feel the soul! Lift the being of the soul to its heights. You stand now before God to offer unto God your being. Feel this! Ask God anything. This is your soul speaking with God.

You've prepared yourself and your surroundings and givings to God. Ask first that the highest entity of the angels surround you. Ask of a god or of the one great God to honor your requests. God interprets feelings as the language of all entities. God is absolute perfection, all-consuming love, power, intelligence, and organization of the one God of all gods of all existence. It's more than one soul can understand. The heavens are beyond explanation. All perfection, form, design, energy, and life emanates from this being. The life in all worlds, in all strata — all is love beginning in God's thought. The soul is not afraid of death because it will never die! The soul bends to no other, for the soul is all! Nothing in life is needed but your soul.

How does this new spirituality affect me?

Let your voice reflect your new awareness with a softness and a lower, calmer tenderness. Let the face smile as you greet others. Let the eyes show genuineness and aliveness. Stand tall and feel the light of God shining from your soul. Let your movements be serene, gentle, direct, and truthful from straight, strong thought.

From this moment, you will give to others the love within through kindness. You are a Child of God. Behave as if God were before you this moment. Hold back gossip and inconsistent banter of no value. Let your words be directed by a strong, purposeful mind. Your words tell of the qualities you hold. Let your words reflect your communion with God. Let your clothing, surroundings, cleanliness, and orderliness be in dignity and reverence to the Almighty God.

Do your labors with a cheerful heart. One day, you will see yourself as others see you. Let each moment reflect the new awareness of your glorious soul. Give your life now to this purpose. This life now holds no pretense, no affected movements, no falsehoods, nor any hidden disgusts. This will be the genuine aliveness of your true soul.

The pure wonderment of the living soul is shining for all to view. Don't let the low miseries of others bring you to the same state. By opening your heart to God, you are opening the soul to beauties inconceivable. Know this: Your calm reactions, your gentle demeanor, and your wisdom-filled words softly spoken are now part of you. Be the most wonderful soul you are capable of becoming. You are a god emerging from a chrysalis.

Why You Should Choose God

Almost everyone has done things they are ashamed to admit. How does this affect the growth to God?

Growth of the soul is inhibited by indulgences of the lowly carnal movements and actions. The soul is to seek higher lifting toward God and the glorification of the soul. It's a form of shamefulness to demean oneself. This is to be abhorred. The soul within will seek the higher path. Keep your soul surrounded by your strength of grace.

Why would anyone want to do the right thing over immediate returns?

In each action requiring response, you are given a choice. You can take the path of the lazy and uncouth, or you can don the demeanor of reverence. Some might cower or perform actions in courage. Some might sacrifice for others or indulge in avarice. Taking the higher stance may not bring you to immediate pleasures, acclaim, or rewards. When the soul presents unto God, it's the light of the soul that is seen. The soul may be adorned in magnificence to meet the one God, but the soul will be seen in all authenticity. Nothing is hidden from God.

So little needs to be done to do right action on Earth, yet people often choose the slovenly, saddened ways of debauchery and perversity.

Choose the way of God and at the time of revealing your true self to God, you can stand high and proud before him to unveil your strength and courage. The virtues of the soul will be built during your life. You might be born on Earth as a lowly soul and leave the body as a soul of greatness.

Life on this Earth is a gift from God. The purposes are few: Lift the thought in the mind to grow to God. Lift the feelings of the heart to grow to God. Help others in their growth. The aloneness of the soul is to be cherished because in this solitude, the soul can best communicate with the one God.

Give gifts of kindness to others, even strangers. Use powerful thought to send love to these people. Build treasures in your soul. These will be utilized in future lives. It's so important that you know the power you hold to grow to God. No one will applaud your telling only truths, of not thieving from another, or not weakening the soul by substances not wanted in the body. No award will be held for you on this Earth by not hurting through words and actions. Build the strengths in your soul. Know you are strong and brave. No one will cheer because you are kind and thoughtful. No one may know of your difficulties and your triumphs. But God knows. The angels know. You know.

How do we develop character?

To be free in thought, place no restrictions in the mind. The mind is to be free from fear and tribulation. Only in this state of freedom can the soul begin building individual character. Fear binds the freedom of mind and thought. Anger constricts free thought. Pain constricts free thought.

When the order of the mind is free to think as it chooses, it turns toward whatever thought makes the soul feel happiest. You can train the mind to think strong thoughts and send these thoughts into the atmosphere. Sound has influence over the mind's function, as does forced wakefulness. Sleep regenerates the mind. Let the heart and mind rest to recuperate for higher function. Prayer to God will focus thought using emotion to strengthen the thought.

Care for the mind as you would care for the body. Let no one invade the thought process. This is the individual's reasoning power. Let the soul express through the body and mind. This must be free, unaltered expression. Reason may enter the mind to constrict varied expression as the body ages, but the mind must not be encumbered. As the soul integrates with the body, character and values are measured as the mind's goals. The word of God may be used to attain this.

The values you have acquired at the end of your life are well earned. Perhaps they have been known but not practiced. You know in your soul what is right to do. Follow this rightness. You may grow rich by swindle or coercion, but these are temporal pleasures. The knowledge that you have done right by God and the angels is a better reward. If you don't know what is the right action to take, ask for guidance. Souls will not be punished for intentionally doing wrong, but they might not be given the most lofty heavens after this life.

To not thieve, you are given discipline of the soul. When the main gifts of honor are bestowed, the soul may lift to a heaven most high. Be the finest person you can be while on Earth. For each quality of the soul you struggle to obtain, others will be opened to you. To be cheerful and lighthearted in the face of adversity, you are given compassion. When you reach to lighten other's burdens, the compassion within you overflows. The world needs these qualities. A world of chaos is what Earth is becoming.

Each of you must look not to others but to building your own soul by integrating higher qualities of the soul into your life. Look at your own soul not as a lowly being but as a magnificent, honored soul worthy of God's mercy. No matter what the soul has done in the past, it is known what you are to attain. From this knowledge on, you are to be worthy.

How do we help others?

Earth is inhabited by souls who need love. A life of any soul needs your feelings of compassion. Picture all souls as healthy and happy. When a soul desires an object and it's given instead to another, if the soul can feel intense joy for the recipient, it has grown immensely.

Expect Miracles

Why don't we get our desires right away?

We want to tell you a story. The great god known as Melenaphut offered to bring a world much beauty. The people of that world were in great anticipation of the god's gifts. They expected lights, scents, colors, and wonders only the gods can create. This god went to the world to bring these wonders.

When he saw the world, he backed away because the world's inhabitants were not ready for the wonders to occur. Yes, they wanted and expected them. They begged and pleaded, prayed and gave thanks. They all gave everything they could in praises to God for this gift.

The time of arrival came and went with no change to their world's beauty. Why? Why did this god plan to come to them but didn't do anything? The reason is that a life of wonder must be earned. It's not to be given without purpose. All things can be given, but the soul must be ready — not in desire, but in actions and thought of the past.

When wonders occur, they are often planned over lifetimes. If miracles are performed before the soul is ready, the wonders swiftly dissipate because the soul is not capable of sustaining them. The mind must be grounded with no erratic movements.

Why are some people rich and successful while others, who may be wonderful souls, wallow in poverty?

Yes, we understand the question. A person in ignorance can live in luxury while another, being in all goodness in thought and action, will live in misery. This is because this was determined before the birth on Earth. When you sit with the angels, you discuss your most important goals in the life to come. The life plan is determined in accordance with the soul's desires. This can be ignored, dismissed, or followed after the birth on Earth. This is a movement of the soul.

The human life on Earth is not to be wasted. It is a gift from God to be in a human body. As you live this life, ask God how you can leave your mark on humanity to make the world a better place. You can do this. You can be the catalyst to change the world into a world of love. Humanity can continue in ignorance and hate or can emerge as a world of God. Life is to be used in God's purpose.

We angels come to those in despondency, pain, and agony, but we touch them only in sympathy to bring solace from the pains. Rise from this. Bring wonders into your life. You are better viewed by angels in light and aliveness than curled in a pit of darkness.

You are to take the first step by opening your heart to feel the love of God. The love will be felt by the entities of the heavens. The most wonderful actions will be enacted from opening the heart to feel, sending forth this love to all around you. Adore the life you are given. Begin from this moment. Know without a doubt that blessings and healings will be fulfilled. This will happen.

Cheryl Speaks About the Angels

How did the angels' appearance and your communication with them change you or your life?

I look at people differently. I see them as souls rather than people. I try to give them more attention, listen to them more intently, and be more understanding because I'm aware of the varied growth levels we are going through at the same time. There's an awareness of people's pain and sadness. Everything is felt more intensely. When I think of the compassion the angels feel as they watch us, it's pretty overwhelming.

We don't always know how people are hurting, what they're feeling, or the sadness they're holding inside. Because of this, we should always go out of our way to be kind. My father, Cortland Gaer, enhanced life for everyone around him every day of his life. I couldn't come close to this, but it's something to work toward.

I think this experience has made me more aware of enjoying every moment of life. My awareness is more expansive. I can look up at the heavens on a starry night and feel as if I could weep with joy. God and the angels aren't just words anymore. They are no longer far away. They are here and alive! They're real and all-encompassing. It's hard to explain the feelings welling inside me when my angels surround me. I feel as if I've opened my soul to God. It's a more profound and sacred feeling than I can describe.

The love of God is a love like no other. Not one soul can know of the magnificence of God. It's unexplainable! When the angels are around me, there is a softening of feelings into what I can only describe as an extreme tenderness. All souls are sweet, delicate, and gentle, no matter what their exteriors.

I've forgiven everyone who has ever hurt me in my life. The angels tell us to not only forgive but also bless those who have hurt us. This might be a little much for this planet. I'm beginning to understand their meanings, though. You bless them deeply so that their souls feel the blessings, and then you send them tremendous love. This frees you and actually brings you joy! You begin to gain insight into the truths the angels are unveiling.

Another change in me is the development of a love for life. Could I be luckier than to have all these angels around me? I know their names and how they look. There's an excitement about life and an aliveness I hadn't experienced since I was a teenager. There isn't a smidgen of worry or fear of death because I know how wonderful it will be. Please, everyone: Let joy and happiness into your lives. Laugh, sing, dance, and delight in everything! Why wait until we get to the heavens? Why not love our lives on Earth?

Do you think that you pray more often now because you receive angelic communication?

Yes, I pray to give thankfulness for anything and everything. It is all silent prayer because my thoughts are known. I pray for the suffering people in the world. These prayers aren't just said; I really feel them. I mean, I *really feel* these prayers!

You know that you only have a certain amount of time on Earth. Why spend even a moment of the time you have here in anger? It just makes you miserable! Why not use those same moments in wonder, love, and happiness? I've known people who have lost their tempers and feel they have to stay in that miserable mood for hours or days. This is just a decision of the mind. You can change your entire attitude in one second! You can choose to be happy or miserable. The angels mentioned that in one of their discourses.

Do you get messages from gods as well as from angels?

Oh yes! Not all gods communicate with people on Earth. We're not the highest entities, you know. A few will give powerful messages for growth to God for the people of Earth. Most (and there are more gods in the heavens than could be counted in a billion lifetimes) do not communicate with us. I was given the name of the god of healing to help someone dear to me. I was told not to repeat the name, as it is not to be bandied about the lower worlds. I've kept that promise. This puts in perspective the sacredness of these celestial entities.

The gods reiterate that prayers and pleadings are to be given to the one God of all gods. I fluff this off, but when it really hits me — the hallowedness and divinity of the words I'm receiving — it's a feeling of incredible reverence.

When were you first aware of angels?

Before the angel visitation, I had an awareness of translucent figures around me all my life, I guess. They were "spirits," I suppose, but were sweet and helpful. As a child, I lived next to Yellowstone River. I was at the river most of the time, barefoot and playing on the shore. A tribe of skinny, scantily clad American Indians were always there with me. I could see through them, so I knew they weren't human.

I was always aware of my guardian angel beside me or above me. She always appeared in a whitish glow of light. As a little girl, I'd go to church with my parents. I could see my transparent, luminous angel sitting beside me. I listened intently, fully focused on the sermons. At age seven, much of my life is a blur, but these were messages from God! I was mesmerized by the sermons.

One Sunday the minister said, "Unless you believe and are baptized, you cannot enter the kingdom of heaven."

The angel beside me whispered in my ear, "Don't believe that, Cheryl. That's not true."

Well, I stood up on the pew and said, "That's not true!" This was the demise of my religion. The minister told my parents not to ever bring me to church with them again.

The angelic visitation was completely different from any of these sightings. This was more magnificent than anything imaginable. The brilliance, the perfection, the awe of this cannot be described!

My life has been dotted with visitations from entities. I have had more "strange" happenings from unseen entities occur in my life than I have time or space to relate. I know this will make me sound batty, but, yes, I often hear my name called by a deep, masculine voice. This is not an interior voice but an exterior one, and so strong and dramatic that I jumped up and looked around the room. He has since told me his name and that he is the voice I hear in the night. This is an extremely powerful angel.

What is it like to channel these words from the angels?

I don't use the word "channeling" because I don't think that's an apt description. It's as if I'm sitting and listening to a friend. Their words are between a whisper and a thought.

I write the words exactly as I receive them and at the same moment I receive them. I don't feel there's anything mystical about it at all. I will tell you that I know these are not from lowly spirits or "ghosts." The angels warn not to ever communicate with the low spirits. The words are completely different from my own thoughts. I'll be thinking about what I'm planning to fix for dinner, and I'll hear, "Cheryl, when people understand the gravity of hard decisions, the empathy of the soul's heart, and the love they can send to the world, they have matured in the soul to the point they can walk with gods and listen with comprehension." Let's see, "Tacos and avocado salad … what?"

It was a long time before I actually wrote down these sacred messages. This came as an interference in my life. The angels were relentless in their communications. Now I look back and think of all the incredibly important messages I've missed because I refused to document them. They told me, "Cheryl, this is why you were born on Earth at this time. This was agreed on before your birth on Earth."

I carefully weighed the ridicule I would experience with an apparent promise to God. Which do you think came out on top? Evidently, I had promised to bring the angel's words to the world before I was born. They told me, "What was promised to the God takes precedence over earthly mentions." Still, I was reluctant to come forward with the angelic messages.

When browsing through a book one day, the page fell open to a Teddy Roosevelt quote: "Far better it is to dare mighty things, to win glorious triumphs, even though checkered by failure, than to rank with those poor spirits who neither enjoy much nor suffer much, because they live in that gray twilight that knows neither victory nor defeat." This was something I needed to read. This may have been the deciding factor to bring these messages to the world. "Dare mighty things." The angel's words are mighty things!

My ancestors have seen and heard angels. This was always something quietly whispered among relatives in the kitchen. This was not something we would tell everyone. Yet here I am giving these messages to the world. It's time for me to stand up and show some courage!

Do you drop everything to transcribe the messages?

Not at all. My life is so busy! When I have a free moment, I might sit down and ask the angels whether they want to tell me anything. They always do, of course. I write their words and don't even read it until later when I type it up. I might go a week or two before I receive the words of angels. I used to stop what I was doing, but now they repeat the words when I'm ready. It's much better!

Sometimes I'll have a question on my mind to ask them. A few hours will go by, and I'll try to remember what the question was that I was going to ask. The angels will say, "You were going to ask 'this question,' and here is the answer." This is one of those moments when I gasp!

You say you receive the words and write them at the same time. How does this work?

The words come almost as a strong thought into my mind. I'm fully aware these are not my thoughts. Often the angels tell me their names. This is the way I've received the words. I recall a time when my daughter and I were living in a little mountain cabin. I had just gotten home from work and I sat down and grabbed a pen and paper to make a grocery list. Roy Orbison was on the television, and my attention was on the music. I looked down at the paper, and the pen was *writing by itself*! Holy cow! I jumped up and went around the coffee table about eight times! What on Earth?

I asked, "Who are you?" as I picked up the pen again.

The pen began moving again in my hand, spelling out, "Release the pen. This is working." I released my hold on the pen, and it wrote: "My name is Mark. The holy angels of God are waiting to write to you. I will get them."

This was unbelievable! Almost immediately, the words came into my mind, and the pen began writing the exact same words. This time, the words were from angels. I'm receiving the messages by two actual methods. I figured that this was good because I wouldn't get my own thoughts intermingled with the words of the angels.

I was shaking as I sat there with my eyes wide open, thinking, "What just happened?" I did not want to be associated with anything occult or mystical or having to do with speaking with "spirits." I thought, "Why is this happening to me? Can't I just be a normal person? This doesn't happen to other people, does it?" Then I thought, "Okay, Cheryl, get your wits about you! This is an actual happening. I'm already receiving the words mentally and this solidifies the messages." I now have a flowing, direct communication with the angels. I made sure I asked for only the highest of the angels to speak with me. I refused to communicate with spirits or ghosts. I was lucky because only the holy angels are giving me these sacred messages.

Is your family supportive of your communication with angels?

"I'm married to an ol' ex-buckaroo and ex-lawman who is a self-described old reprobate and unrepentant sinner! He has a cowboy mentality, which may or may not be endearing to everyone. He's probably the last person on Earth who would have any interest in angelic communications. But he understands I'm part of something sacred and significant, and he's behind me all the way. Sometimes he doesn't understand the significance of what I'm talking about — just kidding! He's an intelligent and jovial man. My husband has the looks and demeanor of a Texas Ranger, which commands respect. Actually, he was a federal marshal. He has a wonderful sense of humor, and he keeps me grounded.

I consider myself as normal as everyone else, and I have my weaknesses and faults, just as everyone else. Not every member of my family shares the same beliefs as I, and I'm fine with that. My beautiful daughter, Gina, is supportive of me. She's highly spiritual, and our belief systems have always been on the same page. This was not taught to her. This is something she knew in her soul. I can't speak for my son because he's a rugged outdoorsman who is involved in his graphic arts and has put spirituality on the back burner. My husband, my children, and my dearest friends are among the highest and most wonderful souls alive.

When angels talk about the war and destruction of humankind, are you afraid?

No, the angels say not to be afraid of anything! Death is never to be feared! Humans will always be on Earth. The angels warn about a short but devastating war that will occur if humankind does not move in a different direction, but this can be changed. The future is dictated by the unified consciousness of humankind. If thoughts are elevated and prayers are given for peace (and really felt), the world could be looking at only wonderfulness! Humanity foretells the future of the world. The angels talk about how imperative it is to lift the quality of thought on Earth! It's necessary that this be done now!

Do you consult the angels on everyday choices?

When I first became aware I could ask the angels anything and they would respond, the first question was, "What are the winning lottery numbers?" They didn't answer. If I ask personal questions, such as "Where did I lose my ring?" they respond with silence. I don't use the angels' words for frivolous endeavors. They seem to only discuss God and celestial entities, stuff like that. I believe they don't want us to become dependent on them for our everyday lives.

People of this world need to grow and develop. Choices are a part of this. The one time they answered a personal question was when I was frantic over the loss of my cat. They told me she was under a metal building. I live in a small town and drove all over looking for a metal building. The only one I found was a Forest Service building. There she was, hiding under the building for shelter! This was unusual for them to answer a personal question, but I'm sure glad they did.

The angels seem to give little worth to money or material possessions. They seem to give no differentiation to whether a person is deceased or alive on Earth. This is because the soul is alive in the heavens. They speak of time on Earth as being distorted. When I ask, "When will 'this' and 'that' happen?" The angels can't relate to Earth's time. In the heavens, time is an infinite and eternal experience with God. Earth's time seems to have no meaning.

They search my brain for words I understand to correspond with their vast vocabulary. Much of what was transcribed was, truthfully, hard for me to swallow. Jesus has a spiritual mother and God is his father? Hell is a place of opulence? We are the recipients of our thoughts? We are the ones who shape the goings-on in the world? I wrote the words exactly as received them. I changed nothing! When I was given names of gods, worlds, and such, I stuck them away in a closet for a year and asked the same questions again. I brought out the written names, and they *matched*!

I stand behind every word the angels have given me. I know without a doubt these are true words. How can anyone, looking around at the natural, perfect order of creation and really seeing the incredible design of Earth and the heavens, not believe in a superior being?

I was told I was chosen by God to bring the words of the holy Angels of the Mallbon to the world. These are sacred messages needed on Earth at this time. These are words I was given not once but multiple times. What began as an interference in my life has become a great honor. All truths have not been revealed. They will come by varied means. We must be open in our hearts and minds to receive them and to be aware of our surrounding angels. These are truly the most sacred angels in all creation.

If you knew how many times your surrounding angels have helped you or saved you, you would be thankful for them at every moment! Your angels want you to enjoy every moment of life. Be as wonderful as you can. Be truly thankful for everything. Lift your hearts to God!

About the Author

Cheryl Gaer Barlow has been communicating with angels most of her life. She attests that the first holy angel of God she ever saw floated through her window to appear before her in an intense blue-white light. The angel reached out to touch her forehead and spoke to her. This was neither a dream nor a vision but a genuine visit from an angel of God.

"We give you the most powerful words given to any mortal," the angels told Cheryl on a subsequent visit. Cheryl was told she had been chosen to bring the words of the holy angels of God to Earth and that this was her life's purpose. Knowing she was part of something spiritual and significant, Cheryl wrote down the words of the angels exactly as she received them. The angels also gave her heightened feelings and perceptions. "I then understood how the soul integrates with the intellect to determine the quality of thought and thus the quality of the soul," she explains. "I felt a refining and a softening into a tenderness I'd never before experienced. I have one foot in the heavens and one on Earth."

Cheryl grew up in Miles City, Montana, and has spent most of her life living in and traveling through the western United States. She now enjoys living in New Mexico with her husband — an ex-cowboy and an ex-U.S. Marshal — along with their dog, their cat, and their horse. In addition to communing with the angels, her other passions include painting and bronze sculpting.

Cheryl Gaer Barlow

Angels Explain Death and Prayer

$16.95 • Softcover, 224 PP.
6 X 9 Perfect Bound
ISBN 978-1-62233-008-9

"We are the angels of the Mallbon. We are meant to tell those of Earth that the death of the body is never to be feared. We help in ways not understood by humanity. We can manifest anything we desire. We can live as humans on Earth. When we absorb the reality of Earth, we work God's wonders in ordinary ways.

"When the surroundings are not in focus or when you feel unable to cope with the people or circumstances around you, be still and ask God for help. God will respond to requests of help by mending emotions with aid from the angels. This is done by being aware of the angels. We surround you and bring you comfort.

"You must, as a human race, lift the quality of thought to the highest level. When the level of thought is low and miserable, it is generated through the entire world. When it is lifted to a level of joy, it lifts all minds. When you know the teachings of the angels, no ignorance will be left in the soul. You will no longer be afraid or in pain. Now is the time to stand with the angels of God and help humankind."

— The Mallbon Angels

Chapters Include:

- The Soul's Path
- The Death of Children
- Meeting God
- Dreams
- Birth on Earth
- Entering the Heavens
- The Joy That Awaits You
- Bonus: Prayer Guide!

RAE CHANDRAN

DNA of the Spirit, vol. 1

Channeled through Rae Chandran with Robert Mason Pollock

The etheric strands of your DNA are the information library of your soul. They contain the complete history of you, lifetime after lifetime; a record of the attitudes, karma, and emotional predispositions you brought into this lifetime; and a blueprint, or lesson plan, for your self-improvement. Your DNA is also a record of your existence from the moment of your creation as a starbeing to your present incarnation. This information is written in every cell of your body.

CHAPTERS INCLUDE:

- Mudras for Activating the Twelve Layers of DNA
- The Awakening of Crystalline Consciousness
- Auspicious Times for Awakening Consciousness
- Angelic Support for DNA Activation

$19.95 • Softcover • 384 PP.
978-1-62233-013-3

32 color pages of mudras and images to activate your 12 levels of DNA

DNA of the Spirit, vol. 2

Channeled through Rae Chandran with Robert Mason Pollock

This companion book to *DNA of the Spirit, Vol. 1* originated with the intention and desire to bring forth understanding to support humanity. Go through this volume while holding a sacredness inside of you, asking that the material be imprinted in your sacredness so that it may become an experience that you will be able to live.

Some of the material in this book is coded, and sincere students will find they can open these codes. Understanding can be received through your own filter and in your own way. This way, you will find the Divine within.

CHAPTERS INCLUDE:

- Auric Imprinting Technique for Healing
- The Number of God
- Reveal Your Life Contracts
- Re-Create Your Life with Your Akashic Records
- Humans Are Creators in Training

$16.95 • Softcover • 192 PP.
978-1-62233-027-0

Light Technology PUBLISHING Presents

DAVID K. MILLER

FIFTH-DIMENSIONAL SOUL PSYCHOLOGY

The basic essence of soul psychology rests with the idea that the soul is evolving and that part of this evolution is occurring through incarnations in the third dimension. Now, to even speak about the soul evolving is perhaps a controversial subject because we know that the soul is eternal. We know that the soul has been in existence for infinity, and we know that the soul is perfect. So why would the soul have to evolve?

The answer to this question is complex, and we may not be able to totally answer it using third-dimensional terminology. But it is an important question to answer, because the nature of soul evolution is inherently connected to your experiences in the third dimension. The soul, in completing its evolutionary journey, needs these experiences in the third dimension, and it needs to complete the lessons here.

—Vywamus

$16.95 • Softcover • 288 PP. • 6 X 9 Perfect Bound • ISBN 978-1-62233-016-4

OTHER BOOKS BT DAVID K. MILLER

1

2

3
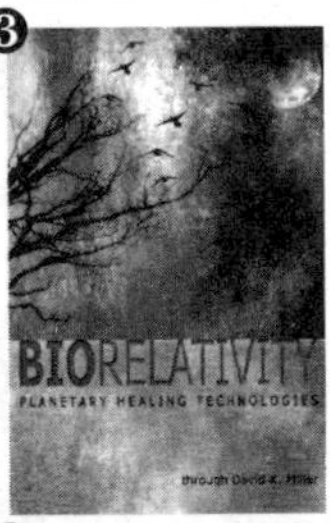

4

5

6

7

8

9

1. **Arcturians: How to Heal, Ascend, and Help Planet Earth**
   $16.95 • 352 PP. • SOFTCOVER • 978-1-62233-002-7
2. **Kaballah and the Ascension**
   $16.95 • 176 PP. • SOFTCOVER • 978-1-891824-82-1
3. **Biorelativity: Planetary Healing Technologies**
   $16.95 • 352 PP. • SOFTCOVER • 978-1-891824-98-2
4. **Raising the Spiritual Light Quotient**
   $16.95 • 384 PP. • SOFTCOVER • 978-1-891824-89-0
5. **Connecting with the Arcturians**
   $17.00 • 256 PP. • SOFTCOVER • 978-1-891824-94-4
6. **New Spiritual Technology for the Fifth-Dimensional Earth**
   $19.95 • 240 PP. • SOFTCOVER • 978-1-891824-79-1
7. **Teachings from the Sacred Triangle, Vol. 1**
   $16.95 • 292 PP. • SOFTCOVER • 978-0-971589-43-8
8. **Teachings from the Sacred Triangle, Vol. 2**
   $16.95 • 254 PP. • SOFTCOVER • 978-1-891824-19-7
9. **Teachings from the Sacred Triangle, Vol. 3**
   $16.95 • 254 PP. • SOFTCOVER • 978-1-891824-23-4

Print Books: Visit Our Online Bookstore www.LightTechnology.com
eBooks Available on Amazon, Apple iTunes, Google Play, and Barnes & Noble

Light Technology PUBLISHING Presents

$16.95

Plus Shipping

ISBN 13: 978-1-62233-017-1
Softcover 256 PP.
6 X 9 Perfect Bound

The Comprehension of the Holy Spirit within the Human Condition

Spirit of Space with Gabriel et al. through Arthur Fanning

TOPICS INCLUDE:

- The force of the Holy Spirit is coming: Are you ready?
- The forty-nine personalities in your chakras are unifying.
- Your soul force is expanding.
- Your birth name and birth date are vitally important.
- Your bones are becoming more fluid.
- The Moon rules the water in your body.
- Gratitude, appreciation, and prayer are essential now.
- Your thoughts: Are they yours or someone else's?
- All religions have the same god, the same idea, why fight?
- And much, much more.

COMING SOON

Permission to Ascend

Spirit of Space with Gabriel et al. through Arthur Fanning

Phone: 928-526-1345 or 1-800-450-0985 • Fax: 928-714-1132